BASEBALL

A Casual Fan's Guide

by

John Yates Britt

www.casualfansguide.com

Baseball – A Casual Fan's Guide

Published by:
CFG Enterprises, LLC
Post Office Box 8125
Calabasas, CA 91372

Casualfansguide@gmail.com

First Printing, 2013

Copyright 2013 by John Britt

Library of Congress Control Number: 2012923359

ISBN 9781625096180

The purchaser and/or user of the book and any related materials assumes total responsibility and risk for use of the book and any related products or services.

Information contained in the book and related materials is intended as an educational aid only.

The publisher or its owners, sponsors, or agents do not assume any responsibility or risk for the use of any information contained within the book, or other materials which could contain inaccuracies or errors, and where third parties could make unauthorized additions, deletions, and alterations without the author's knowledge.

Although the author, the publisher and its owners, sponsors, or agents have done their best to ensure full integrity throughout all media, they make no guarantees whatsoever regarding the accuracy, comprehensiveness, and utility of the work.

www.xulonpress.com

In Memory of

George Horace Britt
(Who Loved the Game of Baseball)

and

Leo White
(Who Loved the Chicago Cubs)

Two of the Most Honorable and
Decent Men I Have Ever Known

TABLE OF CONTENTS

Preface

It is hard to like something if you don't understand it. Millions of people like baseball and have a working understanding of the game. Many millions more know little, if anything, about baseball, and it is for them that I wrote this book. My intention is to provide a plain, simple, and straightforward explanation of the game of professional baseball, so that the people who know little or nothing can understand the game, and maybe even come to like it.

I grew up not liking baseball. Actually, it's more accurate to say that I came to dislike baseball as I was growing up. My dad, however, loved the game; he was absolutely passionate about it—played anywhere and at any level. He had grown up an orphan in rural North Carolina during the 1930s, and I've been told that he was a good pitcher in his early teens. Dad was wiry and agile, sharp-eyed, and he could run really fast.

I wasn't so naturally gifted. To put it kindly, I was a husky child. I also wore glasses from the time I was six—thick glasses, back in the days when there were no plastic lenses. I liked to read, and I was cursed with being left-handed in a right-handed world. Dad didn't see it as a curse. A child of the Depression, he looked at my stout frame and my left-handed throwing and hitting, and he saw a future Babe Ruth (the first great baseball/sports star, the "Babe," who was also large and left-handed). Therefore, he decided that, like the Babe, I should play either first base or right field.

To play first base, I learned that I needed a special glove, known appropriately enough as a first baseman's mitt. Dad found me a left-handed one at a junkyard for a dollar, and after repeated applications of neatsfoot oil that made the glove supple but gave the leather a dark, almost black sheen and a distinctive odor, I slipped the thing on my hand and proceeded to first base to await my fate.

Actually, I wasn't too bad as a first baseman. I had good hand-eye coordination and unexpectedly fast reflexes. Also, it didn't hurt that I could knock the heck out of a baseball, which folks expect a first baseman to be able to do. But I didn't like being the center of attention, and when a batter hits the ball and heads for first base, everyone within sight—on the field, in the dugouts, and in the stands—is staring at you, the first baseman, waiting for you to catch the ball and put the runner out. This can be **TROUBLE**, because if the ball sails past you, or goes into the dirt and you can't dig it out, you want to disappear into the yawning chasm that you hope will somehow magically open beneath your feet.

I thought right field would be better since you are out there alone, but it wasn't. Baseball is a summer game; it's usually hot way out there in the outfield, and there is no shade. Also, it's hard for a kid to stay focused on action taking place far off in the distant infield. If you're lucky, there are small flowering grasses sprouting, oddly shaped pebbles, or interesting cloud formations to divert your attention. On those rare occasions when a ball is hit to you (as you'll read, right field generally has the least action of any area on the baseball field), you have to figure out if you're going to run in, run out, or stand still and hope to the heavens that you can see the ball descending upon you through the glare of the sun. Did I mention it's hot? Whether you're a husky kid or not, the truth is that you're standing out there sweating and thinking about a cold soda or a glass of lemonade.

Bottom line, right field was unpleasant. To add to the unpleasantness, my dad became convinced that I was afraid of the baseball, and that I shut my eyes when it came to me. He was right—that thing stung when it hit you! So one evening when I was about nine, Dad took me into the back yard for a game of pitch and catch, where he'd throw the ball to me and I'd toss it back. Dad thought the practice would increase my comfort level with the ball.

I recall the scene vividly. It was dusk. Dad reared back (remember, he had been a pitcher) and fired the ball at me. I saw it coming straight at my head. I was determined not to show fear, not to blink. I stared at that oncoming ball through my soda-bottle-bottomed lenses, and watched it ride right over the top of my first baseman's mitt, straight into my face! My dad didn't mean to hit me with the ball, and I could tell he felt bad about it. However, with busted glasses, bloody nose, swollen lip, unhappy Mom, and a visit to the hospital, I pretty much decided that I didn't like baseball all that much.

I went on to play organized baseball in my teen years, largely to please my dad, but I never came to love the game with the zest that he had for it; I now realize that I never really understood it. I know firsthand that you can play baseball for years and never really grasp the tactics, strategy, and nuances of the game.

Time marched on, and decades passed. I was living in the Washington, D.C. area in my forties, and slowly, over several years, I started following professional baseball—first on the radio, and then by going to games up in Baltimore and New York—and I found myself being drawn more and more into the game. I also found that knowledgeable baseball fans were friendly, and didn't adopt a condescending attitude if I asked questions about the game. The more I learned, the more I came to appreciate baseball, and I think you will too.

In this book, my aim is to explain the game of baseball in a straightforward way. I try to keep it simple, make it understandable, and describe where things fit into the overall game. A while back, I did a field test with two of my wife's Swiss friends who came to visit us in Los Angeles. All they knew about baseball is that folks dress up in costumes, hit a ball with a wooden club, and then run around a field, while other folks in different costumes chase the hit ball around the field and then throw it at each other. (Oh, and they knew that they were supposed to eat hotdogs!) We took them to a game at Dodger Stadium. I talked them through what they were watching, and about the beginning of the fourth inning they pretty much had a grasp. My point: If I can make baseball understandable to a man and woman who speak English as a second language and were born and raised in the Alps, I should be able to explain it to just about anyone. For the next few hours, I'd like you to sit back, prop your feet up, and let me bring you the game as I understand it.

Chapter 1

An Overview and Some Basic Observations

The Magic of "Three" and its Multiples

There is a mystical theme running throughout baseball involving the number three. Three strikes and you're out. Three outs, and your team quits batting and takes the field to play defense. Three outs for the other team, and the inning (as in "you're *in* it") is over. There are nine innings in a game. There are nine players on the field playing defense: three infielders, covering the three bases, which are ninety feet apart; three outfielders, playing left, center, and right field; the shortstop (to stop the ball "short of the outfield") in the infield generally about midway between second and third base; the pitcher (on the mound in the center of the infield); and the catcher (looking somewhat like a medieval knight dressed in armor), usually crouched down behind home plate. Finally, there are three players who are almost always at the center of the action—(1) the pitcher, who is throwing the ball to (2) the catcher, and (3) the batter (from the opposing team) standing at home plate just in front of the catcher, trying to hit the ball, get on base, go around all the bases, and score a run. At the end of nine innings, the team with the most runs wins. If the teams' score is tied at the end of nine innings, they play extra innings until one team scores more runs than the other and wins.

That's baseball in a nutshell. Those of you reading this right now who know something about the game are saying "yeah, but . . . ." It's the "yeah, buts" that much of the rest of this book is about.

This Chapter gives you background information and perspective. Chapters 2 through 7 give you important explanations of the elements of the game and set the stage for a section of the book where I actually talk you through a baseball game as it is being played. If you are in a hurry and prefer to go directly to that discussion, you should skip to Chapter 8; I have written this book so that you can come back to the earlier chapters and read about the things that are not fully covered in Chapter 8.

Before I move on, would you like to know where all of these variations on a theme of three came from? I don't have a clue, and neither does anyone else. It's one of those things about the game that evolved over time. That's just the way it is, which is not a bad thing. If you think about it, all the games we watch or play have rules that we just accept, without any real idea where those rules came from. Nonetheless, we learn the rules of the game so that we can join in the fun.

Baseball is played worldwide, and players from everywhere come to the United States to play in our professional leagues. There are about 8,500 major and minor league baseball players in the U.S., and some 3,500 are from other countries. Australia, Canada, China, Cuba, the Dominican Republic, India, Japan,

Mexico, New Zealand, Panama, Puerto Rico, South Korea, Taiwan and Venezuela are just some of the nations that have produced professional baseball players. The other 5,000 players come from every corner of the United States—from the snowfields of Alaska (where there's a "Midnight Sun" game that's been played each year since 1906) to the steamy bayous of Louisiana.

Be warned: Folks who come to love baseball sometimes fall head over heels for the game. The best example of this that I can think of is one of the greatest professional basketball players who ever strapped on a pair of gym shoes, Michael Jordan. Mr. Jordan left the hardwood at the absolute pinnacle of his basketball career to play professional baseball. He then spent a year in the minor leagues before returning to basketball. I'd say that's a serious love affair with baseball!

The game I'm going to explain to you is the game that is played at the highest professional level in the United States. It is formally named "Major League Baseball ("MLB"), but often called the "major leagues," the "big leagues," or "the Show." (I'll use the names interchangeably.) My aim is to enable you to go to a big league ballpark and understand what you are seeing.

There are many varieties of baseball that are not described in this book. For example, ballparks for children are smaller, and the games last only six innings. There are baseball leagues for young teenagers, older teenagers, schools and universities, and senior citizens. There are leagues solely for girls and women. There is softball, played with that grapefruit-sized ball that doesn't—some folks say—hurt quite so much when it hits you as a "hardball" does, or sting quite so much when you catch it, and there's slow-pitch softball. There are informal varieties of baseball, generally played by kids on a sandlot, dirt lot, open field, rocky field, hillside, or street. All of these can be played with a ball and a bat, or a stick and a rock, sometimes wrapped in a rag, and the players may or may not have a glove to catch with. No matter where or how the game is played, if you understand the way the pros play the game, you'll likely be able to understand the game anywhere and any way you see it played.

Baseball is Different

Because baseball is different from the other major professional sports in the United States, I think it is useful to highlight these differences. If you think about team sports at their most basic level, they almost all share certain characteristics: you have one team (the offense) that is trying to move an object such as a ball or a puck in one direction on a rectangular playing surface (a field, a court, or an ice rink), with the purpose being to score a touchdown, a basket, or a goal. Meanwhile, the other team (playing defense) is trying to stop the offense from scoring, take the ball or puck away, and then move it in the other direction (i.e., shifting to offense) to try and score.

Baseball is the only major American team sport where there is not a direct frontal assault down the field/court/rink by the offense to score points or a goal. Instead, baseball players score by running around the bases counter-clockwise on the diamond-shaped field, touching each base, and coming back to home plate to score. In that respect, baseball is indirect. Also, baseball is the only major American team sport where the defense has possession and control of the ball (primarily the pitcher throwing to the catcher). Taken together, these factors make baseball **seem** like it is more complicated than the other sports, when it really isn't.

1. Expect the Unexpected

A baseball is a spherical object that has a smoothly textured surface, made slightly uneven by the raised seams of stitching that hold the ball together. A bat is a tapered cylinder; when you look at it lengthwise, it too has a circular or convex surface. During a game, a ball being thrown by the pitcher may come toward the batter at anywhere from about 100 miles per hour down to 65 miles per hour, and the pitcher never throws it at quite the same angle or on the same trajectory, so that the baseball spins differently, if at all, on each pitch. Also, batters may not swing at quite the same speed, force, or angle at any given pitch. So you have two curved surfaces that are uneven or tapered (the ball and the bat), which never make contact at the same speed, force, and angle. As a result, the baseball can and does go flying off in just about any direction after it has been hit. This means that a player has to be ready for any event triggered by wherever that baseball goes.

Also, there is what I'll call the "bounce" factor. Footballs are inflated with air, and they will bounce a fair amount, albeit haphazardly because of their shape—a prolate spheroid, which is a fancy name for an oblong sphere. Basketballs, also filled with air, will bounce predictably if they've been inflated properly; if they didn't bounce predictably, no one could dribble. However, baseballs have a cork core, lightly wrapped with rubber, which means they don't bounce a whole lot, they don't have any "give" to them when they hit something, and they may well carom off a wall or another object in an unexpected direction. Wind and other weather conditions (humidity, aridity, heat, cold) figure into the mix as well.

Baseball history also gives us examples of the unexpected. A hitter is extremely fortunate if he hits even one home run in a game—hitting the ball out of the ball field and scoring a run with one swing of the bat. Nonetheless, one time a hitter slammed three home runs in one game in the World Series—hitting three first pitches in three consecutive at-bats "over the wall," thereby earning the nickname "Mr. October." Another hitter, barely able to stand because of a leg injury, came off the bench in the final inning of a World Series game and hit a game-winning "walk-off" home run. Perhaps the greatest hitter of all time walloped a home run on the last day of the season in his final at-bat before he retired (and no, the pitcher did not serve up an easy pitch to hit).

There is more. It is a pitcher's fondest dream to throw a perfect game, meaning that he doesn't allow any batter from the other team to get on base the entire game. As of October 2012, only twenty-three perfect games were pitched in the entire history of professional baseball, and since 1900 there have been just under 200,000 major league games played. One of these twenty-three games featured a pitcher who otherwise had an utterly unremarkable career. He suddenly came alive, rising up during the 1956 World Series and pitching a perfect game. Forty-two years later, a pitcher on that same team, in the same stadium (who actually went to the same high school as did the 1956 pitcher), pitched another perfect game. A year after that, with the man who threw the perfect game in 1956 in attendance (as fate would have it, he threw out the opening pitch), a pitcher on that same team and in that same stadium pitched a third perfect game. Now that's unexpected, and if you figure the odds, absolutely amazing!

2. Baseball Has No Time Limits, and There is No "Sudden Death"

Unlike any other American professional team sport, there is no clock in baseball, and baseball games vary greatly in length. A fast-moving game can be played in under two hours, but I've watched games that lasted well over four hours. A game can last even longer if the teams are tied at the end of regulation play and the game goes into extra innings. Also, unlike professional football, there is no "sudden death," meaning the game doesn't end in the middle of an overtime period because one team or the other has scored.

3. Player Substitution: When You're Gone, You're Done

For a long time I wondered why baseball players were not "mixed and matched"—that is, why didn't a manager take players out of a game in some situations and then reinsert them later in other situations? Player substitutions are integral to professional football, basketball, and hockey. These games would be very different without the constant mixing and matching that goes on. I watched baseball for a long time, waiting for this to happen . . . and it never did. Finally I confirmed what I had already figured out—once a player is removed from a baseball game, he can't be substituted back in. Professional soccer is the only other professional team sport that I can think of where a player can't come back into a game and play once he has been taken out.

4. Players Come in All Sizes and Shapes

Professional football players have evolved into physical giants over the past half-century. Back in the 1960s, any player over 300 pounds was considered too hefty to play; now 300-plus pound linemen are the norm. Players at "skill" positions, such as quarterback, are now often 6'5" or taller. Not only are the players bigger, they are faster as well. Professional basketball players have always been generally taller than the average athlete, but now they are really tall, sometimes topping seven feet, and more muscular than "back in the day." I think it's fair to say that an average-sized person, unless he has blazing speed, quickness, agility and conditioning, can just about forget a professional career in football and basketball.

In contrast, one of the coolest things about baseball is that just about anyone, no matter whether tall, short, heavy, thin, or even poorly conditioned (of course, good conditioning helps!), can play the game at the professional level. There are awesome professional players that are listed at 6'10" tall, and others, equally awesome, listed at 5'7" (probably measured first thing in the morning on a good day, wearing platform-soled shoes and standing on their toes). I've seen top-flight pitchers with profiles like sumo wrestlers, and I've seen others that look downright malnourished. The point is, just about any physical type and shape can play professional baseball. Good hand-eye coordination, fast reflexes, and a strong throwing arm are physical gifts or skills that seem to be essential. Speed and strength are also prized, and can make a difference in the success or failure of a player's career. However, for lack of a better way of saying it, "baseball intelligence" is the most important asset a player can have. If you watch the best players, it is obvious that they are constantly looking and thinking about what is going on around them in the playing field, and they are making real-time adjustments as the game progresses and circumstances change. What you'll pick up over time is that these are the players who will make the fewest mistakes.

5. Baseball is a Mix of Bright-line Rules, Variations, and Inconsistencies

Professional football and basketball are governed by rules that are precise; one might even say they are stringent in their enforcement, although they are constantly being reviewed and changed by those who oversee such things. An example with professional football would be the rules regarding the use of instant replay by officials to review their calls. Instant replay was on-again, off-again for several seasons, until finally it seems to be here to stay. Rules in professional basketball are even more flexible when it comes to changes. A few years back, in the middle of a basketball season, the powers-that-be suddenly decided that the first round of the playoffs would be extended from a five-game series to a seven-game series. This may sound like a small change, but it has had a huge impact on the playoffs. Also, the rules for using particular types of basketball defenses have been changed more than once to speed up the pace of the game and increase scoring.

By comparison, change in professional baseball has been glacial. Like football and basketball, most aspects of the sport are standardized by rule, and those rules are specific. For example, in any park in major league baseball, the distance between the back of home plate and the "rubber" at the center of the pitcher's mound (the little white rectangle on top of the mound of dirt in the center of the infield) is required to be 60 feet, 6 inches. Same goes for the distances between the bases (90 feet), the size and weight of a baseball (9-9 ¼ inches in circumference, and 5-5 ¼ ounces), and the distance (18 inches) up the shaft of a bat that a player can smear pine tar for a firmer grip.

However, variations and inconsistencies abound. Most baseball teams have the names of the players sewn on the back of their uniform tops, called jerseys. One team, the New York Yankees, has never done this, and for historical reasons, likely never will; the Yankees' archrival, the Boston Red Sox, puts its players' names only on the "away" uniforms. Ballparks differ in size as well. Some hold more than 50,000 fans, others hold about 35,000. Also, the actual dimensions of ballpark playing fields vary significantly—within generally prescribed limits—and they are not designed and built symmetrically. Differences include playing surfaces and the amount of foul territory in any given ballpark. Some of these variations can be traced back to the early days of professional baseball, when the stadiums were built on whatever piece of land was available (for example, the original Yankee Stadium was built on the site of an old lumber yard); other variations evolved because of advancing technology, or were a consequence of changing a ballpark's seating capacity.

One of the most famous examples of a ballpark with unique characteristics is Fenway Park, home to the Boston Red Sox. Fenway was originally built in 1912 on reclaimed mud flats adjacent to the Charles River. Fenway has a host of nooks, crannies, and features that have been given colorful nicknames over the decades. Here is just one famous instance: In the 1930s, Fenway's left outfield wall (to your left if you are standing at home plate surveying the field) was rebuilt and raised to protect passers-by on the street just outside the stadium. This wall, dubbed "The Green Monster" because it is painted an ugly flat shade of green, is 37 feet tall, higher by far than any other left field wall in major league baseball. The Green Monster effectively cuts off the playing field, which otherwise would extend farther out. Although there is some dispute about just exactly how far the

Green Monster is from home plate, there is little doubt that its height has robbed many a hitter of a home run.

6. Baseball Has the Minor Leagues

There was a time in our not-too-distant past when most Americans didn't go to college. People who lived in rural communities (more than half the population) were lucky if they finished high school. As a consequence, instead of recruiting new players from college teams, professional baseball developed its "farm system" of minor leagues that fed new talent into the major league ball clubs. As currently constituted, there are three classes of minor league teams: Class A; Class AA; and Class AAA (called Single A, Double A, and Triple A, respectively). Raw rookies start out in Single A ball, and as they develop, they move up through the system until they make it to the major leagues. Although professional baseball now recruits players from colleges and universities as well as high schools, the minor leagues are still alive and thriving, because almost all the players begin their careers in the minor leagues.

Other major professional sports became really popular nationally only after World War II, in large part because of the advent of television and the need for programming. By then, many of the returning GIs had the opportunity to go to college and get a degree, and they would later send their sons and daughters as well. As a result, from their beginnings, professional football and basketball looked to the colleges and universities for talent, and only fairly recently have they begun investing in "development leagues" for talented athletes without a higher education. These leagues are fairly fluid—meaning they appear and then disappear— because they don't have the community support that many of the minor league teams established earlier with generations of baseball fans in small-town America.

7. The Baseball Season is a Marathon

Professional football teams can play up to 23 games in a season—4 preseason games, 16 regular season, and 4 postseason, including the Super Bowl. That's a lot of intense physical contact among very large men, and it explains why so many professional football players get injured in some way each year. Professional basketball teams play an 82-game regular season, and could conceivably play an additional 28 games in the four rounds of the playoffs. A big league baseball team plays 162 games during the regular season and as many as many as 20 post-season games. Teams may have games scheduled for 8 or 9 days in a row, and then have a day off before they play for another 8 or 9 days in a row. Sometimes teams will even play two games back-to-back on the same day, called "double-headers," which is unheard-of in any other sport!

Baseball players don't take the physical beating that football players do, and the actual contact in baseball is also significantly less than players routinely endure in basketball. However, the steady wear and tear of a baseball season grinds the players down. The season actually starts in mid-February, when players begin to report to their teams' training camps for Spring Training. In the preseason, the teams play a number of practice games to get the kinks out before the regular season begins. The regular season runs from early April until the beginning of October, and the post-season lasts until early November. That is a lot of baseball—about 8½ months worth. The constant traveling between cities and time zones is physically and mentally exhausting. It means living out of a suitcase for days at a time and arriving at hotels in the middle of the night. Moreover, at any moment during a game a player may suddenly be called upon to exert himself to the absolute limit of his physical ability, which can cause serious injury. Taking all of this together, it means the players are worn down by late August—the Dog Days of Summer—and it shows. Since they are all tired by then, part of the challenge becomes who can hold it together to the finish line—MLB World Champions—and baseball immortality.

8. Baseball Can be "Seen" on the Radio

I have tried to listen to football and basketball games on radio broadcasts, and unless the announcer calling the game is absolutely superb, it's very difficult to see in my mind's eye what is occurring at any given moment. I can follow which team has the ball, and see the players moving down the field or on the court, and I understand when they score and which team is ahead. However, it is hard to visualize the moment-to-moment movement and the nuances, because the action is too swift and the movement of the many players is too unpredictable.

However, baseball games can be followed easily on radio broadcasts. There is less continuous movement in a baseball game. Moreover, the position players are generally locked into their playing zones, and they don't move out of their positions very often. Much of the action is between the pitcher's mound and home plate, and when things do happen elsewhere on the field— always suddenly and without warning—the action is easy to visualize because the players are so spread out. As a result, if I hear the game being described on the radio, I can visualize the action and follow along with what is actually happening at the ballpark. Also, while listening to a baseball game, I often do mundane tasks that don't require too much thinking: wash the car, shop for groceries, pick up the cleaning, etc. That way I get on with what I have to do, and lessen the boredom of the chore by listening to the game.

Having said all this, nothing beats actually going to a baseball game and experiencing it live. You see and hear the action as it unfolds before and around you, eat hotdogs and salted peanuts in the shell, drink soda or beer, talk with your friends, yell your head off with all the other fans, and if you're really lucky, catch a baseball hit out of the field of play. I've been to Camden Yards and its predecessor, Memorial Stadium, in Baltimore (where the Orioles play), old Yankee Stadium (Hallowed Ground to a lot of baseball fans) and Shea Stadium (former home of the Mets) in New York, the Oakland Coliseum, (where the Athletics play, and the coldest stadium I ever shivered through a game in), Dodger Stadium in Los Angeles (in a beautiful setting, with palm trees and mountains in the background), and Angel Stadium in Anaheim (extremely clean, but check out the silly volcano in center field that erupts when an Angel player hits a home run). In all the games I've been to, and all the different places in ballparks where I've sat, I have never had a seat where I couldn't see all the action. Of course, the higher in the stadium you are, the better overall view of the field you have; and when I go to a ballgame I want to see and hear everything. The countervailing advantage of sitting down at the field level is that you get to see the action up close and in more detail.

Chapter 2

The Ballpark
(a/k/a "the Yard")

To make it easy, let's start with a diagram of what a baseball field looks like from directly overhead.

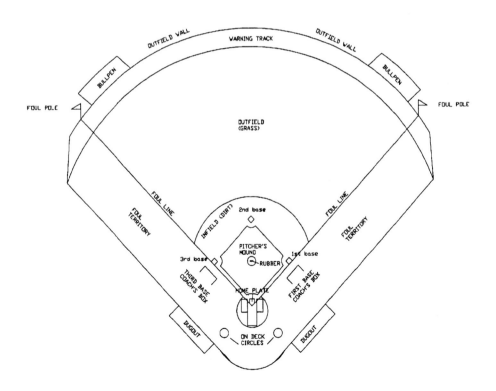

I asked my brother-in-law, a Hoosier raised on a farm, what his first memories were of going to a big league ballpark.[1] There isn't one in Indiana; the closest thing to it is a minor league park in Indianapolis. He told me that his dad took him to see his first game there in the 1950s. Without hesitation, he remembered that what caught his attention was how beautiful, green, lush, and smooth the grass lawn was in the outfield. The same can be said for most major league baseball parks. About the only exceptions are those ballparks that are under a dome, or that are "multi-use" facilities shared with professional football or soccer teams. In the first instance, it is easy to see that the grass isn't real; in the second, the sod gets torn up by the thundering herds of football and soccer cleats.

Moving past the undeniable beauty of the lush emerald expanse in the outfield, let's talk about the layout of the baseball field. It's called a "diamond," for the simple reason that the playing field is shaped like a diamond. At the base of the diamond is home plate, a white, flat, five-cornered rubber slab, flush with the ground, with the longest corner pointing like an arrow away from the center of the ballfield. Home plate is actually shaped like a house when you look at it from inside the diamond! On both sides of home plate you'll see two white rectangular outlines that have been drawn in chalk onto the dirt, with the long sides of the rectangles paralleling the plate. These are the "batter's boxes," where the hitters stand when they come up to bat. Just behind home plate, there is a third rectangle

---

[1] I don't like footnotes because they slow the reader down. Consequently, I've tried to keep them down to a dull roar, and you will see only eight footnotes in this book. However, as a point of clarification, when I refer to a ballpark, or a park, I mean the entire stadium, including the spectator stands. When I refer to a baseball field, a ball field, or a playing field, I mean the actual field upon which the game is played, including "foul territory."

marked in chalk on the dirt, similar in size to the batter's boxes. This is the "catcher's box," where the catcher does his thing. From above, home plate and the area around it looks like this:

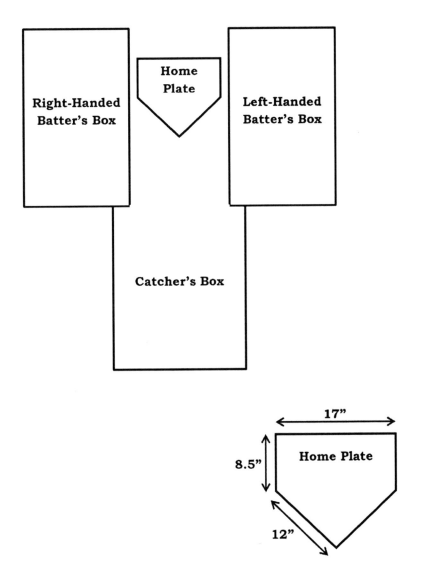

Now, let's stand on home plate and look out on the playing field. Extending out to our right and left are two white chalk lines, which have been laid down all the way from home plate to that fence you see out there in the distance. These are called "foul lines," and they separate "fair territory," from "foul territory." The amount of foul territory varies from ballpark to ballpark. Parks with expansive foul territories—the areas of open ground outside the foul lines up to the edge of the spectator stands—are known as "pitcher's parks," because, as will become apparent later, these parks give the defensive team more opportunities to put batters out than do ballparks with smaller foul territories.

Way, way out there in the field, at the end of each of the foul lines, you'll see a very tall pole, often painted yellow. These two poles are called "foul poles," and they are there to make it easier to see if a well-hit baseball, known as a "fly ball" (because it is flying through the air) drifts off into foul territory before it leaves the air space over the playing field. The foul pole itself is considered fair territory. At the top of each foul pole is a small pennant or flag, so that the players can see the direction the wind is blowing.

Still standing at home plate? Good. Let's turn our attention to the area immediately around you. I've already described the batters' boxes and the catcher's box, and you know they are marked in white chalk on the dirt. In fact, there's a big circle of bare ground that extends out in front of the plate that encompasses home plate and the chalk-defined boxes. Whether it's dirt or grass, anything in front of home plate and between the foul lines is fair territory. You will understand why this is important later in the book.

Look up along the foul line to your right. You'll see that the rather large earthen circle around you features a path that leads off toward a white canvas-covered square, and that the foul line runs right along that dirt path, up to, just outside, and past that square, all the way to that pole I mentioned above. The canvas square is first base. It's about an inch high and just over a foot wide on each side, and it is 90 feet away from home plate. A few feet past first base, the bare dirt ends abruptly at the field of grass (that beautiful expanse that caught my brother-in-law's attention so many years ago) that curves from the foul line on the right side of the playing field to the foul line on the left side. The grass is a demarcation point; it separates the baseball diamond's "infield" from the "outfield." Again, anything between the two foul lines is fair territory, whether we are talking about the infield or the outfield.

In front of the grass, the infield between the foul lines has an expanse of dirt—but the infield isn't all dirt. Inside the arc of dirt is a goodly-sized square area of grass, and at home plate you are standing at the edge of one corner of it. Looking to your right, first base sits at the next corner, ninety feet away. Ninety feet to the left of first base, at the farthest corner of the square from where you are standing (straight out from home plate, close to the edge of the middle of the infield), sits second base. Coming on around to your left from second base, you'll see third base up against the left foul line (90 feet from second base and 90 feet from home plate); you will often hear baseball announcers referring to first base and third base as "the corners." To complete the circuit, coming back to you at home plate from third base is that dirt path, again, with the foul line laid down on it. Just in front of each of the bases there is a fairly small semi-circle of dirt cut into the infield grass square. The three bases, often referred to as "bags," are in fair territory, as is home plate.

In the middle of the square of infield grass is a circle of dirt that rises to a crown ten inches high, called the "pitcher's mound." Atop the mound is a white narrow rectangular plate identified as the rubber, or "pitcher's rubber." One long side of the rubber (the front) faces home plate, with the back facing second base. As I mentioned earlier, the distance from the rubber to the back of home plate is exactly 60 feet 6 inches. During a ballgame, there will be a small cloth bag containing powdered rosin placed at the rear base of the pitcher's mound. You will likely see a pitcher reach down to pick up the rosin bag occasionally; the rosin on his throwing hand will give him better control of the baseball. Also, near the rosin bag will be a mat for the pitcher to clean the dirt off his cleats.

Before we move to the outfield, there are a few more things to notice. First, there are the "dugouts" for the teams. The dugouts are located off the playing field, generally up against or built into the walls of the stadium, and are at least a couple of steps below the playing field so that they don't interfere with the fans' view of the game. With the exception of the pitching staff, the teams sit in the dugouts unless they are on the playing field. A few years back, protective wire-mesh fences with padding on the top and around the edges were installed in front of the dugouts for safety. In some MLB stadiums the home team's dugout is on the first base side of the ball field; in others, it's on the third base side.

Just off the infield, next to first base and third base, are two chalk-marked brackets, or boxes, called "Coaches Boxes." These boxes are where coaches for the team that is at bat are positioned so that they can guide the baserunners. The third base coach also relays signals to the batter from the manager in the dugout.

Behind and to the left and right of home plate, just in front of each dugout, are chalk-marked circles. These are known as the "On-deck" circles, and they are where the next batter awaits his turn. This helps to keep the game moving.

The outfield grass extends from one foul line to the other and from the infield dirt to a few feet short of the outfield wall. Sandwiched between the end of the outfield grass and the outfield wall is a dirt band, or arc, called the "warning track." Like the outfield grass, the warning track runs from one foul line around to the other. It is there so that outfielders who are backing up (or running at full speed toward the wall while looking back toward the infield), and concentrating on catching a well-hit baseball, can know where they are on the field. No one wants to see a player inadvertently run into the outfield wall and hurt himself.

Somewhere next to the playing field—usually, but not always, just past and adjacent to the outfield—you will find enclosed areas for the teams' pitching staffs, called "bullpens." At the beginning of each game, all pitchers except the one who has been designated to pitch (who is on the pitcher's mound), or the guy who was the starting pitcher in the preceding game and won't be pitching in this one, will be in the bullpen. It's likely called a bullpen because when a pitcher is summoned to pitch during a game, the gate of the area will be thrown open and the pitcher will trot out to meet his fate.

The outfield wall curves completely around the perimeter of the outfield, and extends into foul territory on both sides of the playing field. The wall is closest to home plate directly along the foul lines, and arcs out so that it is furthest from home plate in centerfield. Outfield walls are usually made from wood, sometimes brick, and occasionally synthetic material or fabric. Generally they have some protective padding, but not always, and some are higher than others. If they are high, a horizontal line may be painted on the wall to show what constitutes a home run. If the ball is hit higher than the line, it's a home run; if not, then it's a playable "live" ball, meaning that the team on the field that is playing defense can try to get the batter out. Remember the foul poles? If a fly ball hits a foul pole above the outfield wall (or the line painted on the outfield wall) it is a home run—even if the ball then lands in foul territory.

The distance from home plate to the outfield wall is a prime example of ballpark variation; every ballpark is different. The distance from home plate to the outfield wall can vary from around 300 feet to over 350 feet along the foul lines, and from under 400 feet to around 450 feet from home plate to the centerfield wall. As a consequence, it's easier to hit home runs in some parks than it is in others.

Finally, you will notice that there are painted or electronic signs and boards on almost every wall of the ballpark, and there are various electronic boards scattered at strategic locations around the periphery of the ball field. The boards provide lots of information, including who is playing what position, the batting order and who is up at bat, the number of balls and strikes thrown, who is pitching, the pitcher's pitch count, the speed and type of the last pitch, the inning, the number of runs and hits in each inning, and the total number of runs, hits, and errors for the game. Somewhere in the park there will be a scoreboard showing the scores of other major league games completed or ongoing that day. I'll cover all of this in more detail later in the book when we go and watch a baseball game together.

Chapter 3

Equipment—The Tools of the Trade

The Ball

The game of baseball is sometimes called "hardball," as you will appreciate if you ever pick one up. The outer surface, or "skin" of the ball is composed of two hourglass-shaped pieces of leather sewn together with red thread in a continuous line of stitching forming "seams." It looks like this:

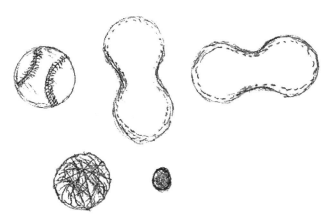

The seams are important because one of the things a pitcher does to throw the baseball and make it do different things (i.e., go up, down, in, out, curve) is to grip the stitching in different ways with different fingers. For example, you will sometimes hear an announcer describe a particular pitch that has just been thrown as a "two-seamer" fastball or a "four-seamer fastball," which are two very different types of pitches.

Like many other little boys, I just had to open up a baseball to see what was inside. I took my pocket knife (this was back at a time and in a place where it was okay for little boys to have such things) and sliced into a worn and scuffed baseball that I found somewhere, looking to unlock its hidden mysteries. The results were disappointing. After cutting through the red stitching, I found a tightly wrapped mass of plain old yarn. Slicing down through the stringy stuff, I ultimately discovered that the core was a cork wrapped in rubber, about the size of the circle that your thumb and forefinger makes when you touch the tips together. As I mentioned previously, the circumference of an official big league baseball has been set by rule at 9-9¼ inches, which is about as big as a medium-sized orange.

Baseballs come from the factory with smooth shiny white skins, but they don't stay that way for long. Before each game, the umpires prepare six dozen new baseballs for possible use, meaning the umpires pull the balls out of the box and intentionally dirty them up. Each ball is rubbed with a special mud, taken from a hidden location somewhere in the wilds of New Jersey and shipped in cans to all of the major league ballparks specifically for this purpose (I'm not making this stuff up!). The mud is to make the surface of the balls less slick and shiny, and by rubbing the balls with the same goop, MLB ensures that the process can be uniform. Also, by having the umpires do it, any possibility of pre-game hanky-panky with the balls is eliminated.

Why are so many baseballs prepared for use during a game? If the ball becomes scuffed or scraped it could change the flight of the ball to the pitcher's advantage, and give him a means to enhance his grip. Also, no two baseballs are exactly alike, and the feel of a ball is important to a pitcher. Some baseballs have higher seams, or even different skin textures, and the pitcher may ask the umpire for another ball if he is not comfortable with the ball that is in play. As a result, you will frequently see the home plate umpire reach into a pouch at his waist and bring out a new baseball to put in play.

Gloves and Mitts

All nine defensive players on the field wear gloves or mitts on one hand to catch the baseball. There are four basic types: catchers' mitts; first basemen's mitts; infield gloves; and outfield gloves. The mitts and gloves are made of leather, with the various pieces sewn, tied, or woven together with leather laces. Mitts, as in "mittens," have a sleeve for the thumb, and a big sleeve for the four fingers (with separate sheaths for each finger inside the big sleeve), whereas gloves have one sleeve for the thumb and one for each finger. The mitts and gloves look like this:

Catcher's Mitt   First Baseman's Mitt

 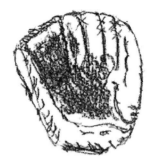

Infielder's Glove   Outfielder's Glove

Let's start with the catcher's mitt. The catcher uses a large circular mitt, about the size of a pie tin, that is designed to: (1) be big enough to provide a decent target for the pitcher; (2) provide added protection for the catcher; and (3) enable the catcher to trap an off-target or errant pitch more easily. All mitts and gloves have a "pocket," which is a built-in depression into which the baseball is funneled. However, the pocket in a catcher's mitt is very shallow, rather like a soup bowl. The catcher actually uses his mitted hand to stop the ball, and his other hand to close over the ball and trap it in the pocket.

Catchers will likely use oversized mitts when they catch balls thrown by certain pitchers, such as pitchers who specialize in throwing "knuckleballs" that will arrive at home plate in unpredictable locations. I've heard a knuckleball's flight path described as looking like that of a drunken moth. In any event, catchers' mitts are thick, and don't bend much. The catcher's hand fits into two sleeves sewn onto the back of the mitt, a smaller one for his thumb and a larger one for his fingers. Since a catcher may catch upwards of 200 pitches a game, many thrown with a velocity of more than ninety miles per hour, his hands take a real beating. Consequently, some catchers stuff extra padding, such as a sponge, inside the mitt for added protection.

The first baseman also uses a mitt, but it looks very different from a catcher's mitt. It is larger than the gloves used by the other players in the field, with a deep and long pocket that actually looks like a vertical gash between the thumb and opposing fingers. This is so that the first baseman can extend his reach to field a throw from one of his fellow fielders, and more easily dig a baseball out of the dirt. The first baseman's thumb goes into a leather sleeve along one side of the elongated pocket, and his fingers fit into the other sleeve.

All other players on the field use gloves that generally look alike, with separate sleeves for the thumb and each finger, and a pocket laced into the space between the thumb and the forefinger. Gloves may have pockets that are solid or "closed," or they may be configured in a "basket-weave," meaning that they are made of strips of leather that literally are sewn and laced together like the strands of a woven straw basket. The main difference between gloves that infielders and outfielders use is the size. Infielders want to be able to field a ball and get it out of their gloves very quickly. Consequently they use smaller gloves than outfielders, with fairly shallow pockets. Outfielders want to maximize their chances of catching a fly ball, so they use larger gloves with relatively deeper pockets.

Pitchers don't want a batter to see the kind of pitch they are preparing to throw, and they use their gloves to help hide the positioning of their throwing hand on the baseball. They also want to be able to field a baseball that is hit "up the middle," meaning it is coming directly back at them (which can be a harrowing experience, to be sure). Consequently, they may use a somewhat larger glove than other infielders, with a closed pocket so that the batter can't see their grip on the ball.

The Bat

Most baseball players have half a dozen or so bats on hand for a game. Some are for back-up, in case their favorite primary bat gets shattered by a pitch. Others are for situational hitting, when the hitter is trying to accomplish a specific task, such as bunting, or for a specific type of pitcher—a fastballer, a finesse pitcher, a knuckleballer, etc. The bats are kept in bat racks in the team dugout, and if you're watching on television you may see a player reach into the rack to select his hitting implement du jour.

By rule, bats can only be, at most, 42 inches long, and are required to be made of one solid piece of wood. Generally, they are made of ash. Way back in yesteryear, they were sometimes made of hickory. However, since the 1990s, more players are using bats made of maple, which is claimed to be more durable. If that's so, then I wonder why more bats seem to be shattering during games than used to be the case.

As I mentioned, a bat is a tapered cylinder, and that rounded surface is achieved by turning a long piece of wood on a lathe. At some major league parks, you can actually watch the process of a bat being made, and if you really want a neat keepsake, you can have one made for "your kid at home" while you watch.

Bats have three distinct parts: the knob; the handle; and the barrel. At the end where the player picks up the bat is the knob. It looks just like a doorknob. The knob is there to help keep the bat from slipping out of the player's hands when he swings (good luck with that). The handle of the bat is the narrow portion of the shaft that gently tapers upward and outward. The batter will grip that portion of the bat with both hands. The upper "business" end of the bat is called the barrel, and it is the fattest part of this long hunk of wood. Bats can be scooped out at the top end of the barrel to make them lighter, creating a dimple; not all of them are rounded off with a smooth curve.

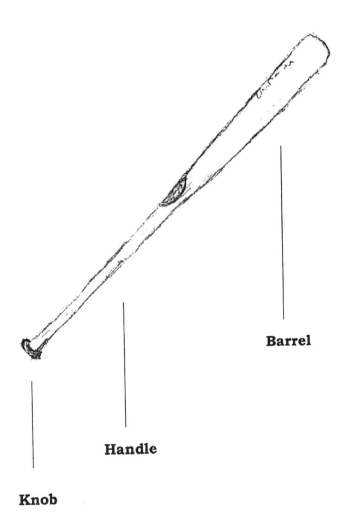

Barrel

Handle

Knob

When I say the business end of the bat, I mean the portion with which the hitter wants to greet the incoming pitched baseball. Somewhere on the barrel is a particular point that is often described as the "sweet spot," and when the hitter swings his bat and the ball hits the sweet spot, you'll likely hear that delicious **"CRACK"** anywhere in the ballpark over the noise of the crowd. It is a sound like nothing else, a sound that batters love, pitchers hate, and fans adore. Why? Because it very often means the baseball has been launched out of the ballpark, and the batter just hit a home run!

Back in the 1920s and 1930s, hitters used heavier bats. Babe Ruth is said to have used a hickory bat that weighed 54 ounces. Most hitters today use bats weighing somewhere between 31 and 35 ounces. Why the change? Bat speed; if a hitter is swinging a lighter bat he can get around more quickly to make contact with the ball. In sum, the batters over the past fifty years or so have traded some power for greater bat speed. The baseball might not travel quite as far, but with the speed of pitching increasing because of a number of factors (including improved conditioning, strength and pitching technique), it's more important to "get some wood" on the ball. Besides, baseball parks are being built with smaller outfields than they used to be, which makes it somewhat easier for players today to hit home runs.

Some final points about bats: First, it's okay for players to use pine tar on their bat handles to enhance grip, but the pine tar can go up the handle only 18 inches. There have been humongous dust-ups in games over whether the pine tar has been smeared too far up the bat. Secondly, recall that the bat has to be made from a single solid piece of wood. Some players have been known to take off the top end of a bat, ream out the core of the barrel, fill it up with cork, and then glue the top of the bat back on. This form of cheating gives the hitter even more bat speed, and is not permitted under MLB rules. Since umpires can't check every bat before every game, there is usually no way to tell if a batter has done this unless the bat breaks when he's using it to hit, and the cork is exposed. A hitter will be punished if he is found to have been using a "doctored" bat.

Batting Gloves and Helmets

Many players wear gloves when they bat to give themselves a better grip and to protect their hands a little. The gloves look like driving gloves with holes in them for ventilation, and they are usually tightened at the wrist with Velcro straps. Some players I've seen go through a lengthy ritual of stepping away from home plate and readjusting the Velcro between pitches. No one seems to know, and the players won't say, whether they do this to ensure the gloves are still tight, or because it gives them a moment to think about what the next pitch is likely to be, or because this is some sort of good-luck ritual. My best guess is that it's some combination of these reasons, and it sure is interesting to watch. Once the players get on base, some keep the gloves on, some take them off and hold them, and some stick them in their hip pocket. It makes sense to keep them on, since they serve the purpose of protecting a base runner's hands when he slides into the next base.

Batting helmets came along in the 1960s. Back then they were optional, but now they are required. They have always been made out of a single piece of colored high-impact molded plastic. Early versions came down to just above the ear, offering limited protection. Over time the helmets evolved, and most players wear helmets that have an earflap on the side facing the pitcher, although some wear helmets with double earflaps. Beginning in the 2013 season, MLB batters will be required to wear a new helmet that offers more protection. Most players keep their helmets on when they are running the bases. The first and third base coaches are also required to wear batting helmets, but they wear the flapless ones.

When helmets first came out, some players clearly thought they were unmanly and a detraction from the game. That was fuzzy thinking. Helmets save lives and careers. A few seasons back, a player I liked was "beaned" with a fastball pitch, meaning that he was hit in the head just above the ear with a ball that sailed in on him at over 90 miles per hour. He was knocked down, badly shaken up, and had to leave the game. However, he was able to come back and play again within a week. I have no doubt that this man would have been crippled or even killed if he had not been wearing a helmet.

The Catcher's Gear

Catchers are the only defensive players to use any equipment other than a glove or a mitt. A catcher will always wear a padded wire mask to protect his face, with a flapless helmet underneath turned backwards (and his ballcap underneath the helmet) to protect his head. Some wear a piece of plastic plating/body armor that dangles from the mask to protect their throats. When you see a close-up of a catcher on television during a game, he usually looks slightly scruffy, as if he needs a shave; he does. Because the catcher is pulling the mask on and taking it off throughout the game, his face would become chafed if he shaved beforehand. Hence, many catchers go into a ballgame with a bit of stubble that helps to protect their skin. A catcher also wears a padded breast protector that straps around his back, and shin guards that extend from over his knees down to his ankles. Even with all of this protective gear, you will see catchers get hit with a foul ball that will necessitate a few moments' break in the game while they recover.

Uniforms

The Players

Professional baseball caps are made of wool felt, except for the brim, or "bill" of the cap. The bill is made of cardboard covered with green or white cotton cloth on the underside to shield the player's face from glare. Inside the ballcap, a sweatband made of cotton runs around the circumference of the cap to keep perspiration from dripping down onto the player's face. All big league ballcaps are constructed in this way.

Each team has its logo stitched onto the front of its players' ballcaps, and the caps are dyed the team colors. Some teams have ballcaps with the bill one color and the cap itself another. Some teams have more than one ballcap, and they switch caps and wear different ones for different games for no apparent reason (perhaps merchandising?). Finally, sometimes the teams wear special caps for special occasions or on holidays.

Generally, the players roll the side edges of the cap bill slightly downward, to help keep the sun out of their eyes. This also helps to protect from the glare of the stadium lights during night games. As kids, we used to achieve an exaggerated version of this by folding the bill in half and jamming it into our hip pocket. Lately a number of players are going in the other direction, flattening the bill out.

Some of the team logos are nifty, and some of the best are the simplest. The interlocking NY of the New York Yankees comes to mind as a team logo that is both simple and hip. A quick historical digression—it was designed by Louis Tiffany in the 1870s for a commemorative medal for the first New York City policeman who was shot in the line of duty. Other teams such as the New York Mets, the Los Angeles Dodgers, the San Diego Padres, and the San Francisco Giants have logos with variations on this interlocking theme.

Ball clubs generally have two uniforms, one for home games and the other for "away" games, meaning the ballparks of other teams in other cities. Usually the uniform jersey, or shirt, and the pants are the same color, but not always. The standard colors are white or gray, but some are pinstriped, and some are blue, red, green, or black—in fact, you'll notice that many teams use the colors blue and red.

Up into the 1960s, uniforms were often made of lightweight wool, because cotton wouldn't hold up to the hard wear-and-tear of a baseball season. Since the 1970s, uniforms are made of polyester, which is more durable than wool, and stretches for ease of movement. However there is a trade-off. Synthetics may hold up better than natural fibers, but they don't breathe as well. To get some sense of how a player must feel wearing a polyester uniform for a day game, you could cover yourself with a large plastic bag, and then run around in 95-degree heat for a few hours while the sun beats down on you. That's why pitchers will sometimes change t-shirts and jerseys between innings.

In the early days of synthetics, many of the team uniforms looked like pajamas and were ugly. Also, many of them had a kind of banded waist instead of a belt with belt loops sewn on, and they made the players look chubby. Over the past two decades or so, a sense of style, often retro, has crept back into the design of the uniforms, and they look a whole lot better now.

Baseball jerseys are most often short-sleeved, but some teams have a jersey that is sleeveless, worn with a colored t-shirt, for warm days. Ballplayers often wear their jerseys a size too large, so that they can have more freedom of movement, and they generally wear t-shirts underneath for insulation, but no doubt also so that the jerseys don't chafe. Some players also wear long-sleeved t-shirts for warmth on chilly days or evenings or for skin protection when they hit the ground while playing.

Each player on a team has a designated number for identification sewn on the front and back of the player's jersey. The practice of putting numbers on the jerseys was started by the New York Yankees back in the 1920s, and the numbers reflected the batting order of the Yankees; for example, Babe Ruth was the third hitter in the order, so he wore Number 3. There probably isn't a professional baseball player alive today who doesn't know that. When fans came to the ballpark to see players they had been hearing about on the radio, or reading about in the newspaper (remember, they didn't have television), they could identify Babe Ruth and the other Yankee players by the numbers. The practice caught on, and the other professional baseball clubs began doing it. Then, most teams added the player's last name on a "rocker" above the number. When a player has made outstanding contributions to his team's success, after he retires, the team may honor him by retiring his uniform number. If so, you will see that number conspicuously posted somewhere in the ballpark.

The current fashion is for baseball players to wear their pants extending down to their ankles. In baseball history, this is a fairly recent fashion statement. Early on, ball players wore long colored socks that extended up to just below the knee to keep the wide-legged baseball pants out of the way; hence the team names of the Boston Red Sox and the Chicago White Sox. Also, if you look at the grainy old pictures of ball players back in the 1920s and 1930s, you'll notice that they wore belts with the buckles cinched off to the side on their hips instead of their mid-section. This was so that the buckle wouldn't dig into their stomachs or get in their way when they were playing.

The old pictures tell us more about the baseball socks as well. To start with, players actually wore a pair of regular socks, and their colored baseball socks fitted over them, made with a stirrup at the bottom that wrapped under the player's foot. During the 1970s, players started pulling the stirrup higher and higher, and at one point in time all you could see was the slim sides of the stirrup, reduced to a colored strip, running up the outside of the players calves. Today, you'll see a few players going for the retro look, wearing socks that extend up to just below the knee, but the socks seem to be one piece as opposed to the layered look of the old days. Funny thing; the guys wearing the high socks often seem to be the same guys with the flat-brimmed caps.

We're down to the shoes. All of the shoes have cleats for traction, and in fact, baseball players call their shoes "cleats." When a baserunner slides into a base, or comes barreling down the line between bases, the defensive player has to watch out for the baserunner's cleats. Back in the day, some of the old-school players would slide into bases "cleats up," meaning their legs were raised with the cleats aimed at the defensive player. The idea was to distract the position player's concentration. Fortunately, this sort of conduct is no longer tolerated.

The Manager and His Coaching Staff

The manager and his coaching staff dress like the players; their caps, jerseys and pants are the same color and design as the rest of the team. They even wear cleats, although they do a lot of sitting or standing around in the dugout or in the bullpen. You'll see a lot of them wearing their team's warm-up jacket or a fleece top with the team logo on it much of the time, especially when it's cold.

The Umpires

There are four umpires on the field during a regular season major league baseball game; the guy behind the catcher at home plate and one behind each base. You won't have any difficulty recognizing them: Stodgy, blocky, substantial, dark, judicial (after a fashion)—these are the words that best describe the umpires' uniforms. They wear gray pants, and if it's cold, a navy blue or black jacket. If it's warm, they wear short-sleeved blue or black collared shirts. The umpires out in the field will normally wear a dark blue or black ballcap with an MLB logo on it. Like the catcher, the umpire behind home plate wears a wire and padded mask to protect his face, with his ballcap underneath turned backwards. Some wear a piece of plastic plating/body armor that dangles from the mask to protect their throats. The home plate umpire also wears a chest protector underneath his clothing. Finally, the home plate umpire will wear shin guards underneath his pants, and special "plate shoes" with protective shields on the front.

That's it for the clothing and gear. Now, let's go through the position players who are on the ball field playing defense.

Chapter 4

The Position Players

An MLB team is allowed to carry 25 players on its active roster from the beginning of the regular season until September 1. On that date, it can expand its roster to 40 players, mainly by calling up players from the minor leagues (the minor league season ends by then). When the playoffs start, teams that have made the post-season must shrink their active rosters back down to the 25-man limit.

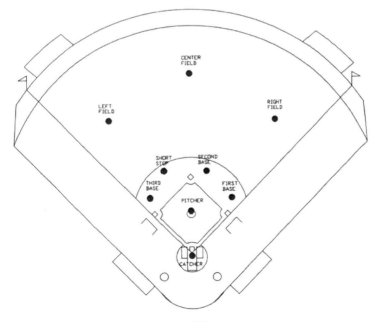

A team fields eight defensive players, and most teams carry eleven or twelve pitchers on their rosters. That leaves a team with slots for only five or six backup players on their active rosters, including at least one backup catcher, for most of the MLB season. Although they can replace a player on the active roster who has been injured at just about any time, teams don't want to do that. Why? If a player goes on either the 15-day or the 60-day Disabled List (generally called the "DL"), the player will be unavailable for those time periods, and the team will have to make do with the best available substitute player for that entire period.

The Infielders

First Base

As I mentioned earlier, first base is located 90 feet from home plate, up the right foul line, sitting at one "corner" of the infield. First basemen are traditionally big hulking brutes, built for power instead of foot speed, but with agility and quickness, which a first baseman needs. That's an over-generalization, and not every first basemen is 6'5" tall, weighing upwards of 240 pounds, but the stereotype bears more than a grain of truth.

It is easy to see why size, strength, and quick reflexes in a first baseman are necessary, considering what he does. He doesn't have to move around much; he sticks close to first base much of the time, waiting to step onto the bag and catch a ball thrown to him by one of the other infielders, so that he can put a baserunner out. The bigger the first baseman, the better the target, and the more likely that he will be able to "snag" an errant throw from one of his teammates. Strength figures in because when they shift over to offense, first basemen are relied upon to be "power hitters." Quick reflexes are important to a first baseman for both his offensive and defensive roles—whether getting wood on a speeding baseball, or reacting correctly and timely in a quickly developing defensive situation.

When there are no baserunners on base, the first baseman usually plays off the bag around ten to fifteen feet, shading backwards and toward the edge of the infield. This field-positioning often enables him to field ground balls or catch line drives (balls that are hit screaming off a bat at astonishing speed with a flat trajectory).

First basemen are usually left-handed (also known as "Southpaws"), so they throw left-handed and catch with the mitt on their right hand. Because the first baseman's throwing hand is toward the foul line, and his body is facing the catcher and is angled toward the infield, he has a half-second or so time advantage over a right-hander in throwing the ball in that direction; and in baseball, half-seconds count. So as not to make right-handers reading this book feel as if they're being discriminated against, I'll hasten to tell you that the same sort of reasoning holds, conversely, for staffing many other defensive positions; as a result, left-handers are largely restricted to playing first base or right field (behind the first baseman) and to pitching.

Second Base

Generally, second basemen are physically smaller than first basemen, with wiry builds, and some of the more famous ones have had fiery personalities. Even when they aren't particularly small men, they're agile. They usually play off the second base bag about fifteen to twenty feet to the right of the bag (toward first base), shading back toward the outer edge of the infield. They are almost always right-handed, which means it takes less time for them to dig a baseball out of the dirt and throw it to first base than it would if they were left-handed. There is usually quite a bit of action around second base, which may explain why second basemen tend to be somewhat high-energy people. If a baserunner gets to first base, and the first baseman moves over to cover the bag to discourage the runner from stealing second, the second baseman will often shift his position in the field closer to first base.

Shortstop

Like the second baseman, the men playing this position were traditionally small and wiry, but not always. In fact, the man who holds the record for the most consecutive games ever played in major league baseball, a shortstop, was 6'4" tall and weighed 225 pounds. He has been credited with having paved the way for other big men to play the position. They are all highly gifted all-around athletes, but historically they did not hit for power. That has definitely changed in the modern era. Shortstops are almost always right-handed, because they are almost always throwing a baseball to first or second base. They generally play midway between second and third base, again shading back toward the outer edge of the infield, and as I mentioned earlier, they are there to stop the baseball "short" of the outfield.

Most people are right-handed, and in this regard, baseball is a microcosm of the general population. Right-handed batters outnumber left-handed batters, and right-handed batters are most likely to hit a ball toward left field. This means that any ground ball will likely go in the general direction of the shortstop. As a result, shortstops generally have the dirtiest uniforms on the playing field because, more than any other player, they will "lay out" to snag a baseball. When you go to a game, you may well see a shortstop make an incredible dive to stop a hit ground ball, and then shovel the ball to the second baseman to put out a baserunner. I've actually seen shortstops dive, grab the ball face down in the dirt, roll over, and in one continuous fluid motion throw the baseball accurately while lying on their backs! Alternatively, you may see a shortstop make an acrobatic leap to catch a ball, and then throw off-balance to put out a baserunner. When either happens, I'd be willing to bet you'll be saying to yourself, "How'd he do that?"

When a baserunner reaches first base and the second baseman shifts closer to first, the shortstop will shift over to cover second base. Also, when a baserunner takes off from first base and tries to steal second, the shortstop will get behind and back up the second baseman if the catcher throws to second base to try to put the baserunner out.

Finally, the shortstop serves as the "cut-off" man when the left fielder or center fielder is throwing the ball back into the infield, meaning that he catches—cuts off—the throw and then throws it to one of the other position players, often the catcher.

Third Base—The Other Corner

Like first basemen, the guys who play third are traditionally big men who are good fielders and can hit for power. Third basemen are almost always right handed, and they have a "gun" for a throwing arm, since they will have to throw a fielded ball with sufficient velocity and accuracy to reach first base.

They usually play off the base about 12 to 15 feet from the left foul line, back toward the outer edge of the infield. However, if they know a batter "pulls" the ball to the left of the infield, they may move over closer to the foul line. The other fielders may also shift their positions depending on a particular batter's known propensities. Like a first baseman, a third baseman will play close to the bag if a runner is on third base; the last thing a third baseman wants is for a baserunner to steal home from third base.

The Outfielders

The three outfielders playing left, center, and right field all share certain characteristics: they are all generally large, powerful men; they can cover ground quickly; and they have strong throwing arms. One of their duties is to move around behind the infielders when a baseball is in play, so that they are in position to back up the infielders and collect any errant throws that get by them. They also back each other up, so that one outfielder will position himself to get to the ball and throw it back into the infield if it gets by the player most likely to catch it. In addition, they have to learn to judge in a split-second where a hit fly ball is going to land—do they run forward or backward, to their left or their right, or do they stay where they are? Then, once they catch the ball, they have to decide in an instant where they are going to throw it—the good ones already have this in mind when they are moving to catch the ball.

Left Field

Again, because most people are right-handed, they hit toward left field. Left fielders need to be fast, so that they can get to a hit ball quickly, but they don't need to have the strongest throwing arm in the outfield since the shortstop and third baseman can cut off and relay the ball. Besides, if a batter hits a ball anywhere in the outfield and it's not caught to put him out, it is well nigh impossible for any outfielder to get the ball to first base before the batter arrives there safely. Left fielders may also be power hitters, but not necessarily. However, if some of the other position players are weak or average hitters, the team may look for someone who can hit for power to play left field.

Center Field

The best all-around athlete playing in the outfield will play in center field. I pointed out earlier that the outfield wall bows out in an arc away from home plate, with the edges of the arc anchored on the foul lines, and the farthest part of the fence way out in the middle of centerfield. That means that the centerfielder has a lot more ground to cover than the other outfielders, so he has to be able to run a long way in a hurry to snag a fly ball, and then he has to be able to throw the baseball he just caught a very long way—sometimes all the way to home plate—to get it to one of the infielders ahead of the baserunner.

Right Field

Right fielders are generally, but not always, the slowest outfielders, and they are often left-handed. Like center fielders, they need to have extremely strong throwing arms so that they can throw ahead of the baserunners and cut them off. The really good ones can throw all the way from the outfield wall to third base and beat the runner trying to get there safely. Also, almost all right fielders can "knock the hide off" a baseball. It is not uncommon for the right fielder to also have played first base at some point in his career, because both positions require similar physical attributes and talents.

Confession Time

My job descriptions for the infielders are comprehensive, but my job descriptions for the outfielders are relatively brief. There is a reason for this. I played in right field for several seasons, but how to get to the correct place at the right time to catch a fly ball remains one of life's great mysteries to me. I've been told repeatedly that outfielders know by the sound of the bat hitting the ball how far it's likely to travel; maybe so, but that sure isn't a gift I was born with, nor a skill that I ever acquired.

As a result, I can tell you that an outfielder made a great catch, but I can't tell you how he did it because I just plain don't know. Having said that, watching as a center fielder makes an over-the-shoulder catch while running full speed toward the outfield wall, followed by his coming to a screeching halt, spinning, cocking, and then firing a dead-accurate throw to the infield as he slumps to the ground is an absolutely beautiful thing to behold. If you want to see this unbelievable act performed, do an online search for "The Catch" and "1954 World Series," and you can watch Willie Mays in action.

Chapter 5

The Battery

W e've gone through all of the various defensive players above, except for two: the pitcher and the catcher. Together these two players form a unit called "the battery," probably because they are the two defensive players who are directly involved in trying to get the batter to strike out. Because the pitcher and the catcher work together most directly, it makes sense to discuss them together and in a separate section from the other defensive players.

Pitching

Pitching wins baseball games. Ask just about anyone who knows anything about baseball what it takes to win, and I bet he will tell you that it's "pitching, pitching, and more pitching." Good hitting is vital, but even with the greatest hitters in the game on your team, you're not going anywhere in the post-season if you don't have good pitching—assuming you even get to the post-season, which is highly unlikely. Because pitching is so important, I'll spend a fair amount of time talking about it.

Unlike professional football, where the head coach and/or an assistant coach generally calls the plays that a quarterback is to run, the manager of a baseball team does not dictate what pitches a pitcher will throw. Consequently, a pitcher has almost unfettered discretion to determine how he wants to pitch to a batter. Often the catcher may advise or suggest, but the pitcher can and will overrule him.

I have heard people say that the hurling of a baseball by the pitcher to the catcher is a glorified game of toss and catch. I beg to differ. It is an exercise in deceit, treachery, cunning, skill, and sometimes intimidation and power. I liken it more to a bullfighter toying with a bull, dancing close with the red cape, hoping to get the bull (here, the batter) to charge the red cape (the pitch). The pitcher hopes to escape unscathed by getting a strike, and ultimately getting the batter out. The difference is, of course, that unlike the bull, the batter can win the contest.

Outstanding pitchers come in all shapes and sizes, and with different talents. However, the really good ones share certain common traits: they're smart, and they've got the nerves and cunning of a cat burglar. They also have the ability to remember what pitches worked best against a particular batter they've faced in the past, while simultaneously retaining the mental toughness to quickly shrug off a rough outing, or the fact that the immediately preceding batter just hit a home run off them.

"Power" pitchers rely primarily on their fastball to strike batters out. They occasionally throw a slower pitch of some sort, generally known as an "off-speed" pitch, that may move, or "break,"[2] to keep a batter guessing; once

---

[2] A generic term encompassing several types of pitches that move away from their initial trajectory before they get to home plate. Some types of pitches break more than others, and some break closer to home plate than others.

in a while they will throw an "inside" pitch, meaning that they send the ball whizzing across home plate at upwards of 95 miles per hour, close enough to the batter to intimidate him just a little bit, back him away from the plate, and make him tentative. The power pitcher throws these off-speed and inside pitches so that he can achieve his main aim—to throw the baseball by a batter so fast that he can't react quickly enough to hit it. Some players remain power pitchers for their entire careers and have been successful major league pitchers well into their forties.

Most MLB pitchers start out with the ability to throw a fastball upwards of 90 miles per hour, but their arms are slowed by the ravages of the Road and Father Time. When this happens, they often continue to pitch successfully by joining the ranks of the pitchers who rely almost exclusively on deceit, known as finesse pitchers (traditionally and less elegantly known as "junk-ballers"). These pitchers will still throw their version of a fastball, but it may not get out of the low-to-mid 80 mile-per-hour range. However, their off-speed stuff is so much slower that the batters still have a hard time figuring out what is coming at them. Regardless whether he is a power pitcher or a finesse pitcher, variations in velocity, pitch placement, and trajectory are tools that all pitchers use.

The pitcher is **THE** great unknown variable in a ballgame, meaning that a team never quite knows what its pitcher is going to do on a given day. Will the pitcher be "on," and able to get the batters out, or will he be having an off day and unable to get out an old blind mule? And it's not just young rookie pitchers who have this problem; veteran pitchers destined for the Baseball Hall of Fame can get knocked around on any given outing. Factors that can influence a pitcher's performance include: whether it's a day or night game; atmospherics (whether the air is humid or dry, or whether there has been a rain-delayed game with intermittent sprinkling, in which case his arm and shoulder muscles may have tightened up); whether it is late or early in the season (early on, the pitchers generally dominate; late in the season they may be tired, and the batters have a tendency to come on strong); whether the pitcher has been or is injured (including such things as a blister on the finger of a throwing hand); whether the pitcher is tired, sick, had a bad night before the game, or is dealing with personal issues; whether he has good fielding support from the position players; whether he's getting good run support by his team's batters; and/or whether the other team batters are just lucky that day, and are able to get wood on his pitches.

In fact, a rookie pitcher may sometimes trump a seasoned veteran pitcher. Many, if not most, of the batters on an opposing team will have seen the veteran pitch before. They will probably have faced him multiple times, so they know his "stuff." If he's having an off day, they may knock him around. However, no one has likely seen the rookie pitch before (unless they batted against him in the minor leagues), so his propensities are unknown—for a little while.

Remember that the batters a big league pitcher faces are, quite literally, the best in the world. Most of them have been hitting a ball or some other flying object with a stick since they were old enough to walk, so getting one of these guys out is not easy. It's always fun to watch a good team face a rookie pitcher his first time up to the Show. The first couple of times through the batting order, the rookie will likely dominate the hitters. But look over toward the dugout of the opposing team and you'll see (and I'd bet the ranch on this) the players, the manager, and the various coaches draped over the rail of the dugout's front barrier fence, watching every move the kid is making on the mound: does he "tip" or "signal" his pitches (meaning whether he does something different when he is about ready to throw a particular type of pitch, such as tug on the bill of his cap, slightly shrug a shoulder, or cock his neck ever so slightly); does he throw the same type of pitch in the same circumstances against different batters; and so on. About the third time through the batting order, they'll start to hit him, partly because he's running out of steam, but mostly because they've figured him out.

With the above as background, keep in mind that the pitcher has only one goal in mind—to get the batter out. To accomplish this goal, the pitcher needs to get three strikes on the batter, or get the batter to hit the ball so that the batter can be put out. If the batter hits the ball, he can be put out if (1) a defensive player catches the ball before it touches the ground, (2) the batter/baserunner does not get to first base before the first baseman retrieves the ball and steps on the bag (in what is known as a "force play", as in "forcing the runner out"), or (3) a defensive player touches the baserunner with the hit ball (after it touched the ball field in fair territory, and was then recovered) when the baserunner is not safely on a base. The pitcher needs to get three outs to "retire the side" and end the other team's at-bats in the inning.

A pitcher has three ways to get a strike on a batter, but they somewhat overlap, as I'll explain. The first way is to throw a pitch through the "strike zone" that the batter either swings at and misses, or lets go by. If the umpire behind home plate sees that the pitch is in the strike zone, and the batter lets it go by, he will call out that it is a strike (hence the term, a "called strike"). The second way for a pitcher to get a strike on a batter is to throw a pitch that will be outside the strike zone, that the batter takes a swing (or a "cut") at and misses. The third way for a pitcher to get a strike is for the batter to hit the ball into foul territory—regardless whether the ball was inside or outside of the strike zone.

There are some tweaks on the foul-ball-as-a-strike rule. If the ball doesn't go outside of the foul lines until it sails or skitters past first or third base (remember, there are umpires standing just behind those bases who will make that call instantly), it is a fair ball. If the hit ball crosses over into foul territory before it passes first or third base, it is a foul; and once it hits the ground in foul territory, it is a strike. However, if one of the players on the other team catches the ball in the air outside of the foul lines, even if he falls into the stands or the dugout while doing so, the batter is out.

Also, the foul-ball-as-a-strike rule is only true for the first two foul balls the batter hits; from then on, the foul balls don't count against him. This means that a batter can end up having a very lengthy at-bat—so long as he can keep getting his bat on the ball that has been pitched. Batters can stand at the plate and make the pitcher throw 12-15 pitches, taking a strike every once in a while, and a ball every once in a while, and fouling off pitch after pitch—and may end up by getting either a hit or a walk (more about the batter later). This has the effect of wearing down the pitcher by running up his pitch count.

Here is where you should be asking yourself, "What the heck is the strike zone?" Remember that the shape of home plate is an irregular pentagon that looks like the outline of a house if you are standing anywhere inside the foul lines of the ball field looking toward home. The strike zone is an imaginary three-dimensional field that rises vertically from home plate, with its outer edges being the sides of the plate. I think of it as a force field, or a beam of light, coming up from the plate. Using your imagination, if you take your hand and wave it over the plate, you are cutting into the strike zone, and—go with me here—if you plunge your arm straight across the plate, your hand and arm will come out of the strike zone on the other side. What I just described looks like this from above:

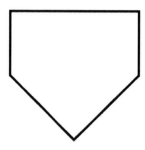

The edges of home plate are the outer borders of the strike zone.

Now that you've got that down, here comes the fun part. Although the strike zone never changes horizontally (meaning that it always goes from one outside edge of home plate to the other), it changes vertically with each batter. The strike zone extends from the mid-chest area of a batter down to his knees. So, if a player is 6'4", his vertical strike zone will be much bigger than that of a player who is 5'8". To add to this, you'll notice that a batter crouches into a batting position when he's awaiting a pitch, so that his strike zone can shrink even more. Consequently, a pitcher can throw a baseball in the exact same spot over home plate that might be a strike for one player but a ball for another player. Again, we are looking to the umpire behind the plate to make the call as to whether or not a pitch is a strike, so you can see that there is room for interpretation—and disagreement—among the pitcher, the catcher, the batter, the umpire, and the managers of the two contending teams, not to mention the fans who are never shy about airing their views of the matter. Here is what the strike zone looks like from the side and from the front:

Strike Zone

Any baseball that the pitcher hurls toward home plate that is outside, above, or below the strike zone (yes, the ball can cross home plate and still not be a strike) is called a "ball," which has a specific meaning in this context. Each at-bat is measured in three strikes and four balls; another way of saying this is that each batter gets three tries to hit the baseball in the strike zone (with foul balls described above being like a wild card), and the pitcher may get to throw four pitches that are outside of the strike zone—which the batter can swing at if he so chooses. If the batter takes (doesn't swing at) these four pitches (balls), before he strikes out, he has earned a "walk," which means he gets to walk to first base for free, and the pitcher has to start all over to try and get the next batter out.

This is a "what you're going to see" book, not a "how to" book. Consequently, I am not going to tell you exactly how the pitcher places his fingers on the baseball to make a pitch, or how he pushes the ball with the palm of his hand toward home plate, or how he torques his arm in such a way as to make the ball spin in certain ways. Truth be told, you're never going to see any of that anyway sitting up in the stands. What you will see is the pitcher going through his throwing motion and firing the ball in toward the catcher, and what the baseball appears to be doing from the time it leaves his hand until it slaps into or goes skimming by the catcher's glove, or gets hit by the batter.

There are a series of formalized movements that a pitcher must make when he's getting ready to throw the baseball, and every pitcher has his own style; regardless, the pitcher must throw from either the "set" (or "stretch") position or the "windup" position. If a pitcher is throwing from the set position, he starts by coming to a still position facing one of the corners, toward first base if he is a lefty, and toward third base if he is a righty. Alternatively, he may throw from the windup position, so that he starts his throwing motion from a still position facing home plate. Either way, the pitcher must have at least one of his feet on or touching the pitcher's rubber (remember, that flat rectangular piece of rubber at the apex of the pitcher's mound), and he must bring both hands up, meeting at his chest, with the hand holding the ball nestled in the gloved hand.

The pitcher is supposed to hold this position for at least a second. He will look in toward the catcher, who will be signaling what type of pitch he thinks should be thrown. The pitcher may slightly nod in agreement, or swivel his head in the universal language of no. This pantomime conversation may go on for two or three signals, until the two men are in agreement.

If the pitcher is pitching from the set position, he draws himself up and "cocks" his body; if from the windup position, he will rear back—sometimes dangling the ball behind him for an instant. Either way, some pitchers hold their position for a slight pause, while others fluidly continue to move, lifting their leg closest to home plate and swinging their throwing arm to catapult the ball forward as they engage in a controlled fall down the front of the pitcher's mound. As the ball leaves the pitcher's hand, the falling motion is halted when the pitcher swings his trailing leg forward, leaving him standing almost at the front base of the mound. The set is a more efficient throwing position than the windup because it doesn't entail the extra movement and time required to rear back before throwing. Also, the pitcher is already facing at least one of the bases. Consequently, if there are baserunners aboard, the set is the preferable throwing position because it makes base stealing more difficult. Nonetheless, many pitchers prefer the windup throwing position because they think its rhythmic movement helps with their pitch velocity and accuracy.

Now, let's go through the basic types of pitches and see what they look like. (The images below are exaggerated for emphasis.)

Fastball (also known as a **Four-Seamer Fastball)**— the pure (traditional) fastball will fly "straight down the pipe," meaning that it will not curve up, down, left, or right, but will fly straight toward the catcher, generally at a speed somewhere between 90 and just over 100 miles per hour—assuming that a pitcher can throw it that fast. That description is actually a little bit misleading, since the ball will have a slight arc as it leaves the pitcher's hand and travels to the catcher's mitt—just like any other object that is catapulted through the air (due to gravity). This pitch is sometimes called a four-seamer fastball because a pitcher grips all four seams of the ball when he throws it. Also, the pitcher can throw a fastball inside or outside, high or low. The fastball is the bread and butter of the power pitcher. The pitch looks like this:

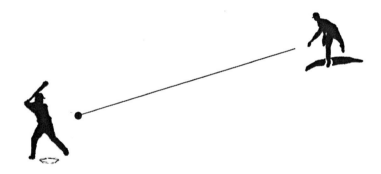

Sinker (also known as a **Two-Seamer Fastball)**—The sinker literally sinks at the end of the pitch. To the batter, the ball looks like it is coming across the plate in the strike zone; and then the bottom drops out of it, and it sinks several inches in the strike zone below where the batter expects it to be. It is sometimes called a two-seamer fastball because a pitcher grips only two seams when he throws it. Some pitchers specialize in throwing the sinker, because if the batter hits it, he generally connects with the top part of the baseball, knocking it downward; as a result, the baseball usually skitters across the infield as a ground ball, making it easier to put the batter out. Here is what a sinker looks like:

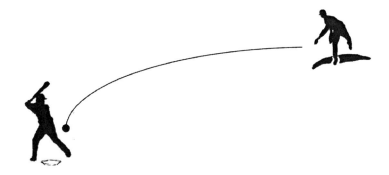

Split-Finger Fastball (also known as a **Splitter)—** The splitter is a slower pitch that, like the sinker, breaks downward as it closes on home plate and may actually hit the plate, or even hit slightly in front of the plate, as it comes in to the catcher. I have been told that catchers hate this pitch, since they have to dig the ball out of the dirt and may jam their fingers and thumbs while getting control of the darned thing. Like the sinker, the splitter causes hitters to connect with the top part of the baseball, leading to a ground ball. Here is the splitter:

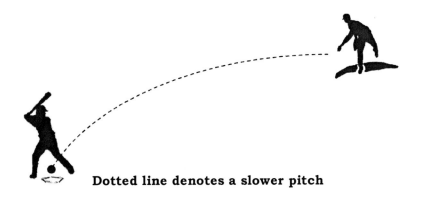

Dotted line denotes a slower pitch

Cut Fastball (also known as a **Cutter**)—The cutter is a fastball that breaks, or curves, sharply to the left or right just before it gets to home plate. It is a very nasty pitch that is difficult to hit, and one phenomenal pitcher that I know of has made a career out of throwing just this one pitch. The cutter looks like this:

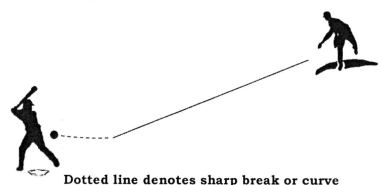

Dotted line denotes sharp break or curve

Curveball—The curveball moves three dimensionally, meaning that it not only arcs up and then down as it leaves the pitcher's hand and heads toward home plate, but it also angles to the left side of the plate (if thrown by a righty) or to the right (if thrown by a lefty). It, too, is a type of pitch that is generally known as a breaking ball because it breaks or moves before it gets to home plate. A **Screwball** (also known as a **Screwgie),** is a pitch that breaks in the opposite direction of a curveball—so, the screwball would break to the right side of the plate if thrown by a righty. My personal favorite, a good curveball is a wicked, wicked pitch. Ladies and gentlemen, I give you the curveball:

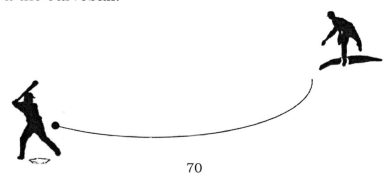

Slider—The slider looks like a fastball to a hitter. Problem is, the pitch starts to slide sideways and down as it comes across the plate, slithering right out of the hitter's range. The slider is also a breaking ball. I've heard the slider described as something like a two-dimensional curveball, meaning that it breaks less than a curveball. Here is the slider:

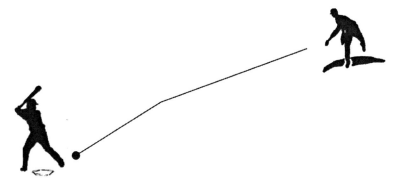

Off-Speed (also known as a **Change-up**)—Before throwing the ball, the pitcher grips it in such a way that it actually comes out of his hand from 10 to 15 miles per hour slower than a fastball. This pitch messes up the timing of the batter, and he ends up swinging too early at the pitch. The trick to throwing the change-up is for the pitcher to make it look to the batter as if it is a fastball, or one of his other pitches (remember, deception is essential). The off-speed pitch also may or may not break sideways or downward. The batter may be confused when he sees this pitch; however, you will not be.

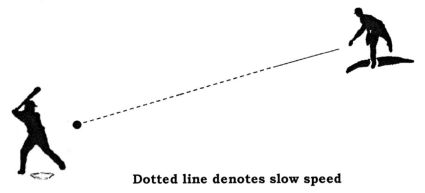

Dotted line denotes slow speed

Floater (also known as a **Knuckleball**)—Because of its alternate name, you'll not be too shocked to learn that this pitch was originally developed by a pitcher who threw the ball using his knuckles; however, these days most pitchers throw it by gripping the ball with their fingertips and digging in their fingernails. The pitcher actually throws this pitch in such a way that the ball has no spin to it; consequently, the wind controls the ball. As I told you earlier, the knuckleball comes toward the batter looking like a drunken moth, and it is absolutely impossible to know where it will cross home plate—assuming that it does! The catcher will use a special oversized mitt when working with a knuckleball pitcher. Knuckleball pitchers are specialists; the floater is the pitch they primarily throw. If they are on, meaning that their floater is working, they are essentially unhittable; if they are off, the opposing team will feast on their pitches.

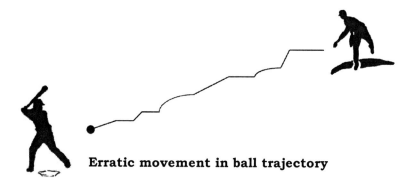

Erratic movement in ball trajectory

These are the basic types of pitches, and there are variations on some of these pitches. One variation is the **slurve**, which is a combination of a slider and a curve. So as you can see, there are many ways to throw a baseball. Most pitchers haven't mastered all the pitches that I've described above, but some don't need to if they have a really good pitch of a certain type. Also, a pitcher may attempt to throw a certain pitch, and not get it right. For example, he may try to throw a fastball low in the strike zone, but instead he "hangs it" high across the middle of the plate—which is not a good thing if you are the pitcher, but is a very good thing if you are the batter.

Now that I've described the types of pitches, let's see what an at-bat looks like. I can't say a "typical" at-bat, because there are thousands of variations on how an at-bat can play out. But here is an at-bat you might see.

A power pitcher is on the mound. He throws "heat"—the speed of his fastball pitches is in the high 90s. In addition to his dominating fastball, this particular pitcher has a good sinker, and a nasty slider. The batter is a power hitter, so we have power against power. The first pitch is a curveball. The batter knows that the pitcher is not likely to start off with a fastball, since the batter might drive it right out of the park, so he holds off swinging, or "takes" the pitch. The ball ends up not crossing the strike zone, so the "count" is 1-0, meaning one ball and no strikes.[3] The batter is now "ahead" of the pitcher, meaning that the batter has the advantage, and that the pitcher may modify what he otherwise might throw as his next pitch.

The pitcher decides to throw a sinker. Again the batter takes the pitch. The ball drops to the ground just behind home plate and just in front of the catcher, so that the catcher has to dive down to scoop up the ball. The pitcher is now behind 2-0.

The pitcher doesn't want to walk the batter, so his next pitch is a fastball inside—in the strike zone, but very

---

[3] The count on a batter always starts by listing the number of balls first (e.g., 0-1 [no balls, one strike], 1-2 [one ball, two strikes], 3-2 [3 balls, 2 strikes]).

close to the batter. The batter was waiting for a fastball thrown down the middle of the plate, but he was out-guessed. Because he anticipated a certain pitch, he was already swinging the bat around when the ball came in; consequently, he caught the ball with the narrow part of the bat barrel and hit it foul. The count is now 2-1. The batter is still ahead of the pitcher in the count, but now the pitcher can throw a fastball, because the batter isn't quite as sure what's coming next. Nonetheless, the batter thinks the next pitch will be a fastball he can hit, and readies himself for it. Sure enough, the pitcher "grooves" the pitch right down the middle, and the batter connects with it solidly. The ball flies out toward left field, but the left fielder runs to the outfield wall, leaps high, and catches the ball at the top of the wall to put the batter out. You probably won't be able to see it from the stands, but if you were close enough you could watch the pitcher breathe a sigh of relief.

You may have noticed that the first couple of pitches are particularly important. If a pitcher can get ahead in the count, he then has the luxury of throwing a higher-risk, higher-reward pitch—a pitch that is less likely to be a called strike, but one that is tougher for the batter to hit. If the pitcher can stay ahead of the batters throughout the game, he is probably having a good outing. Conversely, if he continues to get behind in the count, he is probably going to get "knocked out" of the game sooner rather than later.

Let's turn to one of baseball's great mysteries: the "balk." What is it? To begin with, a balk is not one particular action; it could be a whole host of things that a pitcher does or does not do. The overarching concept is that the pitcher should not make certain motions or take certain actions once he has begun his windup. Why? A balk may disrupt the batter's timing and concentration. More importantly, it could affect the baserunner(s) already on base. Whether or not the pitcher's balk is intentional, it has the effect of tricking a baserunner—it will hold a baserunner close to a base in order to lessen his chances of getting to the next base, or home, without being put out. To allow the pitcher to fake out a baserunner like this would give the defensive team an unfair advantage.

Here are some examples of a balk. The pitcher makes a motion toward one of the bases without taking his foot off the rubber—that's a balk. The pitcher has gone into his set with his hand holding the ball inside his gloved hand, and he takes the ball out of the glove without making a pitch—that's a balk. The pitcher drops the ball—a balk. The pitcher throws a pitch while the catcher is outside of the catcher's box—a balk. You get the point.

Balks are fairly rare, and when one happens, chances are you won't actually see the pitcher balk; what you will see is the home plate umpire call a balk, and you will then see what happens as a result of the call. What does happen? Nothing happens if no one is on base; in fact, a balk won't be called if no one is on base. However, if any baserunners are on base, they will be awarded a free trip to the next base—or home, if the runner is on third base. This can have a real impact on the outcome of a game. I've actually seen a pitcher balk in a run from third base in a game that was tied in the bottom of the ninth inning, thereby losing the game.

I have watched on television as a balk has been called, and then I have watched the replay, and even in slow motion I am not sure I could tell you that I saw the pitcher balk. I am not alone. I've actually asked people who have played baseball at a very high level to describe a balk for me, and I have heard different things from just about everyone I asked. Players actually on the playing field may not see the pitcher balk, or if they see it they won't know it's a balk, and the pitcher may not even realize he committed a balk. It is very possible that the only person on the ball field who saw the pitcher commit a balk is the home plate umpire, because he is staring directly out at the pitcher, watching his every move. The umpires behind first and third base may not see it, because they are focusing on the batter to see if he swings his bat too far and should be called for a strike (which I'll talk about in just a bit), and on any nearby baserunners.

Leaving the balk, when you go to a game you will probably see a number of different pitchers being substituted in. Up until the late 1960s, pitchers often pitched a complete game. That changed after 1968 when MLB decided that pitchers had become too dominant. To balance the odds for the batter, MLB decreed that the pitcher's mound would be lowered. Previously, the pitcher's mound was from 15 to 20 inches high; after 1968, the height was capped at 10 inches. That doesn't sound like such a big deal—but it changed the game of baseball entirely. Before the reduction of the mound, a pitcher was essentially throwing downhill at the batter, and he could conserve energy. After the change, he was throwing with a flat trajectory, which is far more tiring.

Nowadays, it is extremely rare for a pitcher to pitch a complete game, and pitching specialties and sub-specialties have evolved as a result of the lower mound. Collectively, the pitchers are called the "pitching staff," and generally there are eleven or twelve pitchers on a pitching staff. The pitcher that begins a game is called the "starting pitcher," or the "starter." A baseball team will normally carry five or six genuine starters on its staff, but that number varies throughout the regular season and the playoffs, and the "pitching rotation" gives them several off-days between starts.

Other developments over the past several decades have included the tracking of a pitcher's "pitch count," and the use of radar guns to track the velocity of a pitcher's throws. If you are watching the game on television, you might get a shot of the pitching coach clicking his counter as he intently watches the pitcher. When a pitcher gets up above 90 or so pitches, the pitching coach will look for signs that the pitcher is tiring. Other signs that the pitcher is wearing down are when his velocity begins to drop and when his accuracy begins to fade.

The starting pitchers are viewed as the best pitchers on the staff, and some are real divas. These are very competitive men, and they jockey to be known as the "Number One Starter," meaning that they are viewed as the best on the team's pitching staff. The starters will try to go for seven or eight innings, but if they are having an off day, and get "knocked out" of the game early, they will be replaced by the various relief pitchers: The "middle relief" pitcher, who hopes to go in to give a couple of good innings, will be followed by the "setup" pitcher, who comes in to pitch the seventh and eighth innings. During a game, a pitcher can be replaced, or relieved, at any time by another pitcher if (1) he has pitched at least one complete at-bat, or (2) the pitcher is injured. For example, a pitcher is brought in as a reliever at the beginning of the seventh inning, and he pulls a groin muscle or throws out his arm after his third pitch. Under those circumstances, the pitcher can be relieved, and the new pitcher can finish up with the batter. Speaking of injuries, starting pitchers do get hurt during the season. When this happens, relievers may step up to start until the regular starter recovers.

Finally, if the game is close, the "closer" will come in, sometimes late in the eighth inning but most often in the ninth inning. The closer usually has one dominating pitch. Probably the greatest closer who ever played the game had one killer pitch, a very nasty cut fastball that he threw in the high 90s. His cutter came in on the hands of the batter, and got in his "kitchen"— high inside where the batter couldn't hit it, yet still in the strike zone. When the batter tried to fight the pitch off, he usually caught the ball with the narrow part of the bat barrel, shattering the wood. Every batter this pitcher faced knew exactly what he was going to throw, but that didn't seem to help them one little bit. This pitcher dominated opposing batters for over 15 years— and he did it with just that one pitch.

With all of this in mind, just how does a pitcher get credited with winning a game? Basically, if the pitcher pitches through at least the fifth inning and his team is ahead, stays on top, and wins the game, then that pitcher is credited with a win. Conversely if the other team is ahead and wins, he is charged with a loss; and even if his team comes back to win, the best he can do is to be credited with a "no decision." If the pitcher leaves the game with men on base, and the other team goes ahead and wins after he leaves the game, he gets the loss. If a middle reliever comes in and holds the lead, he can be credited with a "hold" if he stays in for three innings (although MLB doesn't officially recognize a hold); however, if the reliever gives up the lead and his team loses, he is charged with the loss. If a closer comes into a game with no more than a two-run lead and holds on for the win, he is credited with a "save;" if he allows the other team to tie or to score the "go-ahead" run, he is said to have "blown" the save. Decades ago, starting pitchers might have as many as 30 wins in a season; these days, a 20-game winner is thought to have had an outstanding season.

You will hear baseball announcers and fans refer to statistics when they talk about players and teams. An important statistic, and one of the ways that a pitcher's performance is evaluated over the course of a season, is his Earned Run Average ("ERA"), the number of runs that the pitcher gave up to the opposing team, or that the pitcher "earned," for the innings he pitched. The lower the ERA, the better the pitcher performed. An ERA of 5.0, or an average of five earned runs per nine innings, would obviously not be very good, while an ERA of somewhere in the neighborhood of 1.5 would be outstanding. In any event, now when you hear someone ask, "What's his ERA?" you'll know what he is asking and why.

Catching

The catcher is the only defensive player that is facing the field, and as a result, he has a better overall view of the playing field than his teammates. He crouches down behind home plate much of the time, and from that vantage point he sees everything. Good catchers are very smart and have prodigious memories: they watch and remember batters' tendencies, such as whether a batter is a contact hitter who merely tries to get on base or a power hitter who wants to wallop the ball out of the park; whether a batter has good "plate discipline" or will swing at bad pitches; and whether the batter hits differently if someone is already on base. Armed with this knowledge, the catcher will suggest pitches to the pitcher; in fact, some catchers see it as **THEIR** job to call the pitches, and they can become annoyed if the pitcher ignores their suggested pitches too often. Also, the catcher will sometimes suggest that the fielders shift their positions on the field to where he thinks the batter is likely to hit the ball. Consequently, the catcher is often called the "field general."

Occasionally you will see a catcher turn, get the okay from the umpire, and then trot out to the pitcher's mound. There, he and the pitcher will have a brief conversation about how to pitch to the next batter. Often, they will converse with their gloves/mitts covering their mouths, so that no one from the other team can read their lips and get a handle on what they are saying.

However, when a batter is standing in the batter's box, the catcher has another way of suggesting pitches. Once he goes into his crouch, the catcher takes his throwing hand and slides it down between his legs in front of him so that no one but the pitcher and his teammates in the field can see, and then (1) signals the type of pitch he thinks is best, and (2) where he wants the pitcher to place it. For example, let's say he wants the pitcher to throw a fastball down and inside (close to the batter's side of the plate and down around his knees). The pitcher and catcher will have previously agreed as to what number of fingers means what pitch to throw, and if they decided two fingers is the signal for a fastball, that is what the catcher will signal. If he wants it inside, the catcher will point his fingers in that direction. If you are watching the game on television, you may see that some catchers actually use white nail polish on the fingers of the signaling hand so that the pitcher can see their signals more clearly.

If the pitcher doesn't like the suggested pitch, you'll see a slight sideways movement of the pitcher's head—the universal sign of "no" (this is also known as "shaking the pitch off"). If that happens, the catcher will keep suggesting pitches until the pitcher moves his head slightly up and down—the universal sign of "yes." Alternatively, the pitcher may go into his windup, which lets the catcher know that the last pitch he signaled is about to be thrown.

You may be asking yourself how the pitcher and catcher keep baserunners from the opposing team, or watchful members of the opposing team in the dugout, from stealing their signs. For example, what if a baserunner hit a double to begin the inning, and he has been standing out on second base watching a pitcher strike out a couple of batters? Good question. It is not illegal under baseball rules for an opposing team to steal signs, but it is considered bad form, and bench-clearing brawls have resulted from it. Also, you can expect a pitcher to retaliate against the opposing batters if he thinks that is happening. However, when a pitcher and catcher think this is happening, the very first thing they do is change the signs; what had been a fastball sign becomes a curveball sign, etc.

The catcher will also know his pitcher, and will work with him so that the pitcher gives his best performance. In addition to sharing a batter's tendencies and suggesting pitches, a catcher will calm the pitcher when he senses that the pitcher is too excited or upset, and he will slow the pitcher down between pitches if he thinks the pitcher is becoming tired. As the game is progressing into the later innings, and the manager is thinking of replacing or "pulling" a pitcher, he will often ask the catcher if the pitcher is running out of steam. As a courtesy, the manager may also ask the pitcher if he is tiring, but he knows the pitcher's preference is to stay in the game!

Catchers are position players, and unlike pitchers, who usually pitch once every five games or so (more often in the playoffs), a catcher can play almost every game if he is healthy. However, a catcher's health is not a given; the position he plays is the most physically demanding in baseball. Remember, he crouches down for every pitch and his legs and knees get tired; he jams and scrapes his fingers and wrists digging foul balls, errant pitches, and breaking balls out of the dirt; and he gets hit with foul balls on his mask, his arms, his legs, and in other places that really hurt. In addition, a baserunner barreling into home plate from third base may slam into a catcher with the aim of knocking the baseball out of his hand so that the runner can score (yes, that is a legitimate tactic). Teams carry more than one catcher on their rosters, so a backup can substitute for the starting catcher if he is injured. Also, a pitcher will often ask to be paired with a catcher he prefers.

In my opinion, the catcher is the best overall athlete on the field, and many can—and do—play multiple positions extremely well. In addition, top-of-the-line catchers have cannons for arms, enabling them to hurl laser-like throws anywhere in the infield to put a baserunner out. Catchers are also valued for their batting prowess, and many of them are power hitters.

Managers take advantage of this athleticism. Late in the regular season, a manager may give a catcher a game or two off from catching, especially if his team has secured a spot in the post-season. However, the manager will likely play the catcher at another position so that he retains his bat in the lineup. This gives the catcher a chance to rest tired legs while ensuring that he doesn't lose his sense of timing for taking live-game pitches. It has the added benefit of giving some other tired or slightly injured player a day off as well, and gives a backup catcher a chance to play.

Chapter 6

Batting—When a Team Plays Offense

We have already covered bats, their size and what they are made of, and how heavier and lighter bats are used for different purposes. Now let's talk about what a player does with that hunk of wood. In a nutshell, a batter can get on base in a variety of ways when he:

- Hits or bunts the ball;
- Earns a walk by "taking" four balls during his at-bat;
- Gets hit by a pitch and is awarded first base by the umpire; or
- The umpire calls a third strike, the catcher does not catch the ball, and then the catcher is unable to throw the batter (now baserunner) out before he reaches first base.[4]

A batter does not necessarily get a "hit" just by hitting the ball with the bat, because the word has a special and specific meaning when used in the batting

---

[4] This can only happen in certain circumstances: when no base-runner is on first base; or the team at bat has two outs—regardless whether there is a baserunner on first.

context. In baseball terminology, a hit means that a batter has struck the ball with his bat and that the ball either (1) landed somewhere in fair territory on the ball field, allowing the batter to get on base without being put out, or (2) landed somewhere over the outfield wall but within fair territory (i.e., within the parameters established by the foul lines that form the boundaries of the ball field), which would be a home run.

With respect to (1) in the preceding paragraph, there are different kinds of hits—some with interesting and descriptive names—depending on where the ball goes:

- The batter can hit a ground ball, or a "grounder," that skitters through the infield between the defensive players ("through the gap") into the outfield, or that an infielder bobbles, or "boots;"
- He can hit a "pop fly" or a "dink" (when the bat doesn't connect squarely with the ball) that one of the infielders loses in the sun (or wind, or stadium lights) and drops to the ground;
- He can hit a screaming "line drive" that is too "hot" for an infielder to handle;
- He can hit a "comebacker" that bounces off the pitcher and caroms off in a weird direction;
- He can hit a "Baltimore Chop" by swinging downward with his bat so that the hit baseball bounces hard and high off hard-packed dirt in front of home plate, and over the heads of the infielders (Baltimore, one of my favorite cities, has a long and interesting baseball history, and I encourage you to look into it further.);
- He can hit a "Texas leaguer" or a "flare" (also called a "bloop," or a "bloop single") that flies just over the heads of the infielders and lands in front of the outfielders;
- He can hit a ball that flies over the head of an

outfielder that has come in too close to the infield, allowing the baseball to roll all of the way to the outfield wall if one of the other outfielders is not backing him up;

- He can hit it off the outfield wall;
- He can hit a ball that looks to be foul, but curves back into fair territory before it hits the ground;
- He can hit a grounder that stays in bounds until after it skitters past one of the bases in fair territory, and then bounces over into foul territory; or
- He can "bunt" the ball (described in detail a few paragraphs below).

The common thread here is that once the batter hits the ball, for it to be a "hit" he has to get to first base safely before the defense can recover the ball and throw it to first base and put him out.

Batters hold a bat in different ways. They all use both hands, and a right-handed hitter (who hits from the right side of the plate, looking in from the pitcher's mound) will grip the lower part of the bat with his left hand, and his right hand will grip it a few inches higher. Conversely, left-handed hitters do just the opposite. Also, if the batter is "choking up" the handle, putting his hands higher up on the bat, this will shorten his swing, and since he won't be generating as much power as he would if he held the bat closer to the knob, the ball won't travel nearly so far. Contact or "slap" hitters are more likely to hold the bat this way.

Hitters' stances vary widely as well. Some hold the bats with their arms reared back at shoulder height with the bat almost vertical, while others hold their bats chest high with the bat sticking straight out behind them, almost horizontal. Some have their legs spread wide, while others have a "closed" batting stance with their legs close together. Some swing the bats round and round while they await a pitch (as a timing mechanism), while I've seen others twirl their bats in tight little loops with the bat cocked behind their ears (I've come to think they do this to distract a pitcher and affect his concentration). Some crouch so low that you think they'll fall over backwards when they swing (which decreases their strike zone), while some stand almost ramrod straight. Some batters move their front foot half-a-step back as the pitcher unloads, and then bring their foot forward again as they move into the pitch (another timing mechanism).

What is really cool (although the batter wouldn't appreciate it nearly as much as the person watching him) is to see a power hitter swing at a pitch with all of his might—and miss it. If the hitter has put everything he has into the swing ("swinging for the fence"), he'll spin around like a top with such force that he may even fall down. As an onlooker, you cannot help but speculate just how far the baseball would have traveled if the batter had made contact. Along those lines, you'll frequently see a batter start to swing at a pitch, and then try to stop his swing before his bat crosses the front edge of home plate, to avoid incurring a strike. If that happens, the home plate umpire may consult with the appropriate field umpire by pointing to him (to the first base umpire if the hitter is a righty, or to the third base umpire if the hitter is a lefty) to make the call as to whether the batter "went around." In addition, the catcher may ask the umpire to consult with a field umpire—but the plate umpire does not have to oblige.

While we're talking about righties and lefties, be aware that some players are "switch hitters," meaning that they can bat from either side of the plate. Generally, these players are better hitters from one side of the plate than the other, but their ability to switch does add another dimension to their game. Say, for example, the pitcher is a lefty. Even though a player may be naturally left-handed, he may switch around and bat right-handed for that pitcher. Why? It is harder to hit a baseball that is moving away from you, and a left-handed pitcher's pitches will naturally move away from a left-handed batter. The same holds true for a right-handed pitcher and a right-handed batter. Also, be aware that a switch hitter can change from batting left-handed to batting right-handed at any time, including during the middle of an at-bat.

The Bunt

A bunt achieves the same goal as swinging a bat (that is, getting the bat on the ball) but instead of swinging the bat like a club, the batter comes out of his batting stance, faces the pitcher, and slides his top hand up from the bat handle to a place behind the barrel. Essentially, he is pushing the bat at the ball, and at least in theory, he should be able to guide the ball where he wants it to go. Generally, a manager will not call upon power hitters to bunt; most likely it will be the leadoff batter, a weak hitter, or the pitcher who will be called upon by the manager to "lay down a bunt." The manager will relay his signals to the first or third base coach, and that coach will give the batter the sign to bunt.

If all goes according to plan, the batter will be able to guide the bat barrel to make contact with the ball, which will knock the ball downward and into the infield. In that perfect baseball world, the bunted ball will dribble to the right or left of the pitcher's mound, slowing down as it goes, until the ball slows or stops equidistant from the catcher, the pitcher, and the closest infielder. While the nearest defensive players are scurrying to scoop up the baseball and throw it to the first baseman to put the baserunner out, he will be making tracks for first base, hoping to "beat out" the throw. Sometimes, if there is a baserunner already on base, and the team wants to move that baserunner to the next base, the batter will bunt with the almost certain knowledge that he will be put out at first base; this is called a "sacrifice bunt." If there is a baserunner on third base, and there is only one out in the inning, the batter may try a "sacrifice squeeze" bunt; the batter sacrifices himself so that the runner on third base can score. A variation on this is known as a "suicide squeeze," where the baserunner on third base runs for home plate as soon as the pitcher goes into his windup. If the bunt is good, the baserunner on third has a good chance of scoring; if not, well, the name says it all.

However, things don't always go according to plan. Bunting seems harder than it looks, or than it is in my memory from when I learned how to do it, because all too often things go awry: The bunted ball may pop up in the air, making it easy pickings for the defense; the ball may travel too far and too fast, allowing the defender to quickly field it and put the runner out at first base; or the bunt may go foul. Also, some players never seem to have learned that they are supposed to keep their fingers away from the ball on the hand they slide up the bat barrel, and they expose themselves to the real possibility of serious injury. To be fair to the MLB players, I've never tried to bunt a 95 mile-per-hour fastball coming straight at me, so it's easy for me to criticize.

A final note on bunting: Remember when I was discussing pitching and I told you that a batter could have a very lengthy at-bat by fouling off pitches? That doesn't apply to bunts. Let's say a batter tries to lay down two bunts in a row. If the bunts go foul, they are strikes. However, if the batter then attempts a third bunt and the ball goes foul, he is out, whether or not the ball is caught. Why? Since it's easier to get the bat on a pitch with a bunt than it is with a swing, it would give the batter too great an advantage in keeping his at-bat alive.

The Batting Order

The batting order, or "lineup" (meaning the order in which players come to bat), is important because a manager wants to maximize his team's opportunity to score runs, and the arrangement of the lineup allows him to do that. The batting order has no direct correlation to the position that a player might play on defense, although, as you'll see below, the requirements of certain of the defensive positions mean that certain position players will typically bat in a certain sequence.

Prior to each game the manager sits down and decides what his batting order for that game will be, tweaking the batting order to best match the strengths and weaknesses of the opponent's starting pitcher, the ballpark's peculiarities (distance from home plate to the outfield wall, size of foul territory—remember, these vary from park to park), and the other team's fielding skills. He will also take into account whether the scheduled opposing pitcher is left-handed or right-handed, for the reason we talked about a few paragraphs ago. Once the manager has made those decisions, he fills out a lineup card with his batting order du jour, and in a pre-game ritual, both managers meet at home plate, exchange lineup cards, and give copies to the home plate umpire.

Once the lineup card has been given to the home plate umpire, only limited substitutions can be made, and the manager cannot do a wholesale reshuffling of his batting order. If a "pinch hitter" is substituted into the game to bat in place of another player, the pinch hitter must take the outgoing player's place in the lineup. The same goes for when a player is injured and unable to continue; the substitute has to bat in the outgoing player's place on the lineup card. The only exception to the rule on not moving players around in the batting order is the "double-switch," which I'll explain in just a moment.

I haven't yet talked about the organization and structure of professional baseball, which I will discuss later. For now, it's enough to say that Major League Baseball is divided into two leagues: the National League and the American League. This is important with respect to the batting order. In the National League ("NL"), the pitcher has to bat, but in the American League ("AL") the pitcher is replaced by a Designated Hitter (or "DH"). The DH rule came into being in the 1970s, when the AL team owners decided that they wanted the teams in their league to be able to generate more offense. The NL never followed suit, opting instead for tradition.

The DH rule sounds like a small distinction between the NL and the AL, but it isn't. Remember, pitchers only pitch every four or five games, so even if they would otherwise be decent hitters, they do not get sufficient game at-bats to maintain their hitting ability. Consequently, if they are in the lineup, they are the weakest link, and a manager must always be mindful of that. Even if a pitcher gets a hit, it's usually a little dink hit that gets him on base. The DH is almost always a power hitter, often a player who has slowed down with age but who can still hit effectively.

Because NL teams don't have a DH and the pitcher bats, teams in that league resort to the "double-switch" to get around having a pitcher bat when they need a stronger hitter in the lineup. Remember when I told you back in the first chapter that once a player is taken out of the game, he's done? Well, when a manager does a double-switch, he pulls two players out of the lineup; the pitcher and a position player. He inserts the new pitcher into the position player's spot in the batting order, and the new position player in the old pitcher's spot. This normally happens in the later innings of a game, when the pitcher being removed would otherwise be coming up to bat, and the position player being removed is sufficiently far away in the batting order that it is unlikely that he would get to bat anytime soon. The down side of the double-switch is that the position player coming in may be a better hitter than the pitcher he is replacing in the batting order, but he probably isn't as good a defensive player as the position player that he will be replacing.

In both the NL and the AL, there is one more twist on the substitution of players. Sometimes late in a game, a hitter who is not a very fast runner will get on base. The manager may replace him with a baserunner who is faster. The downside of this substitution is that the baserunner substituted into the game will have to play a defensive position, unless of course the manager replaces the new baserunner with another player when his team next plays defense. You can see that this can all get very complicated.

The typical starting batting order 1 through 9 will look like this:

1. The leadoff batter is usually someone who does not hit for power. Rather, he is often what is known as a slap hitter: someone who hits solely to get on base. He is usually fast and quick; for

that reason, shortstops and second basemen are generally leadoff hitters. The best ones have really good "plate discipline," meaning they don't hack away at any old pitch that comes in their direction. The important thing is for the leadoff hitter to get on base. So, whether he gets on base by getting wood on the baseball, by "working the count" and taking four balls to earn a walk, or even by getting hit with the baseball (which earns the batter a free "on base") it's all peachy-keen—because the leadoff batter has achieved his goal.

2. The second batter in the lineup is usually a good hitter, optimally someone with a batting average better than .300, meaning that he gets a hit at least three out of ten times at bat. His job is to move the leadoff hitter over to second or third base. As I have heard it explained, NL teams play "small ball," meaning they have an offensive philosophy of "get 'em on, get 'em over, and get 'em in." NL teams traditionally have tried to "manufacture" runs. It makes sense that they would approach hitting and scoring with this philosophy because they do not have a DH, and therefore may have a weaker lineup than their AL counterparts.

3. The player batting third in the lineup will be more of a power hitter. He is up at the plate to get a hit: best case, to hit a home run or a long fly ball that drives in runs. Likely, this hitter will be one of the defensive corners—the guys playing first or third base—or one of the outfielders.

4. The fourth batter is the team's strongest batter. If it's an AL team, this will likely be the DH (alternatively, the DH could be hitting in the number three or the number five spot). The point

is, this batter is up at home plate to swing away, to hit a home run, or at least to drive in some runs from teammates who, it is hoped, have already gotten on base in front of him. For this reason, he is referred to as the "cleanup" hitter. Because pitchers will fear this batter, they may walk him intentionally, or throw him "garbage" in the hope that he will swing at a bad pitch and be more readily put out. Also, the number three batter benefits from a strong number four batter; the pitcher will likely throw strikes to the number three batter (which he can hit) to get him out, so that he won't be on base to score if the cleanup hitter wallops a home run.

5. Another strong hitter, the fifth batter is in the lineup to drive in runs. In fact, the three, four, and five hitters are called the "heart" of the lineup, or the "power alley." Back in 1927, the New York Yankees lineup was so daunting to opposing pitchers that it was known as "Murderers' Row."

6. This is where the power in the lineup starts to tail off. The number six hitter is still a good strong hitter, but he's not as good as the number three, four, and five hitters.

7. A weaker batter, but a good enough position player that the manager wants him on the field for his defensive skills.

8. An even weaker batter, but also a sufficiently good defensive player that he is a regular player.

9. The bottom of the lineup. In the NL, this will almost always be the pitcher. In the AL, this will be the weakest batter that is a regular position

player. I know of instances where position players have become so infuriated when they have been moved into the number nine hitting spot (which can happen when a player is in a hitting slump), that they have refused to play!

When I started following baseball, I wondered why it was important that the lineup be arranged just so. After all, the lineup might start off in the first inning all neatly planned out, but sooner rather than later the first player at bat in an inning will be the number three batter, or the number five batter, or even the number nine batter—which made me think that all of this scheming and planning was for naught. I inquired and I was disabused of this notion. The point of all of this is that the team that is batting wants its batters coming up to the plate in a certain rhythmic order, with repeated power surges during the course of a game. The theory is that over several innings, this will wear down the opposing pitcher and produce runs. It also guarantees that the best batters have a chance to get up to bat the most number of times in a close game with few hits.

Before we move on, let me touch on a couple of statistics that are important in measuring a batter's performance—his batting average and on-base percentage. A hitter's batting average is measured on a percentage scale of 1 to 100. As I mentioned above, if a batter gets a hit three out of ten times that he comes up to bat, he has a batting average of .300 (commonly referred to as "three-hundred;" you would not express it as "point three hundred," or "thirty percent."). In any event, .300 is a pretty good batting average when you consider that a batter will come up to bat three or four times a game. (Remember, a regular season is 162 games long, so that is somewhere around 550-600 at-bats.[5]) Only five players in MLB history have ended a season with a batting average over .400, and the last guy to do so, Ted Williams, did it in 1941. I have heard it said that professional baseball is the only endeavor where if someone is successful only four out of ten times, he will be honored as having had an outstanding career.

Generally, on-base percentage ("OBP") is the number of times a player gets on base by getting a hit, earning a walk, or being hit by a pitch, compared to his total number of plate appearances. This is an important measurement of how good a batter that player is, although it does not necessarily correlate with being a power hitter. A leadoff batter with a high OBP is truly a prized player. Also, because a cleanup hitter is intentionally walked so many times during the season, he will likely have an extremely high OBP.

---

[5] If a batter gets on base by earning a walk, being hit by a pitch, getting a sacrifice hit, or for a couple of other reasons, his plate appearance does not count as an official at-bat. Consequently, a batter may make perhaps 650 plate appearances during a 162-game season, but end up with significantly fewer official at-bats.

Chapter 7

The Rest of the Cast

The Manager

The manager, sometimes also called the "Skipper" (nautical slang for a ship's captain), manages the team. That sounds like a simple task, but nothing could be further from the truth. The manager decides who plays and when, including who bats and in what order, who pitches and when, when a relief pitcher comes into a ballgame, and when a pinch hitter comes into a ballgame. The really good managers are consummate masters of the game; they make their decisions based on decades of experience (most if not all were professional players themselves at some level). Because they have to deal with many different types of egos and personalities, they are practicing psychologists. They have to be able to tell a man that he is going down to the minors; that he is going to sit down for a game; that they are changing his place in the batting order because it's for the best interest of the team; that the player needs to "pick it up," or that he needs to "loosen up." In short, they want to win, and they must work to get the best out of their players—their motivation will always be what's best for their team. If I were going to sum up an

MLB manager's job in one phrase, I would turn to an old saying: the manager is "the chief cook and bottle-washer;" he does it all. It is always easy to second-guess a manager's decisions, and ultimately they all end up moving on, often to another team. But the good ones really make a difference.

The Coaches

In professional football and basketball, the person with the job that is somewhat equivalent to the job of a baseball manager is called the head coach, and his assistants are called assistant coaches. Why isn't a baseball manager called a head coach? The manager of a baseball team manages his coaches and his players, and with the exception of the bench coach, baseball coaches are responsible for directly coaching the players in specific areas and/or skills. In other words, the manager is not himself a coach. The manager generally picks his coaches. Here are the main types of coaches and some of their duties:

Bench Coach: The second in command, he advises the manager. Most bench coaches are very seasoned coaches; sometimes they are former managers. Occasionally a manager will get thrown out of a game because he has become too heated in his exchanges with the umpires over a call or a series of calls that the manager didn't like. If that happens, the bench coach will take over and run the team for the duration of the game. The bench coach is often someone that the manager knows extremely well and is very comfortable with; a man with wisdom and experience that the manager can trust to give good objective advice.

Pitching Coach: He stays in the dugout with the manager during games and advises the manager on pitching decisions, including when a pitcher should be relieved. He also advises a pitcher on how to pitch to particular batters. Consequently, during the game you will see him walk out to the mound to talk with the pitcher; sometimes with the manager, but often by himself. He may also signal proposed pitches to the catcher, who will relay the proposals to the pitcher. In addition, he trains the pitchers and works with them between games to ensure they are ready to pitch their best. For example, if a pitcher is having a problem throwing a particular type of pitch, the pitching coach will work with him to get his mechanics back on track so that he can make the throw properly.

Bullpen Coach: He stays in the bullpen with the pitchers. Remember that I told you that except for the pitcher from the immediately preceding game, all other pitchers remain in the bullpen during the game. The bullpen coach is responsible for getting them warmed up if they may be called into the game to pitch. He coordinates with the pitching coach during the game via a closed-circuit telephone, and the pitching coach passes along instructions as to which pitchers should get warmed up and when they need to be ready to pitch.

Batting Coach: During the game, he stays in the dugout as well, and watches his batters hit. Much of his work is done between games and pre-game, watching the batters swing, and helping them perfect their batting skills. Just about anyone can improve his performance at any endeavor, even if he is a consummate professional at the pinnacle of his career. Moreover, major league batters take hundreds, if not thousands, of swings with a bat every season. Over time, they may develop bad habits connected with such matters as inefficient leg spacing, or how they hold their bat or how they swing. These bad habits can lead to a real fall-off in a batter's production. It is the batting coach's job to look at the batter and analyze what has gone wrong and how to fix any problems that develop. He not only watches the batter in real time, but he also looks at video of the batter at the plate—so he can slow down the action and do a step-by-step review of the batter's mechanics.

First Base Coach: His main job is to advise a baserunner on first base when to stay and when to try to go to second. Along those lines, he tries to help the baserunner keep from getting "picked off," that is, being put out by getting caught too far off first base when a pitcher throws over to the first baseman. Also, it is the first base coach's job to tell a hitter-turned-baserunner whether to keep going to second base if he has hit a baseball into the outfield. In addition, he will relay signals to the baserunners and the batters.

Third Base Coach: He does what the first base coach does, but he does more of it. He coaches the baserunners on second base, and those who left first base when the baseball was just hit and are rounding second base, whether to hold or try to make it to third base. He also coaches the baserunners on third base whether to hold or to go for home. More often than not, the third base coach is the man who will pass in the signals to the batter telling him whether to hit away, to bunt, or to take a pitch without swinging.

The Umpires

As I mentioned above, there are four umpires on the field during a regular season major league ballgame: one umpire behind the catcher at home plate, and one behind each base. The umpire behind home plate is always designated the chief umpire for the game, and he is responsible for calling balls, strikes, foul balls short of the outfield, and whether a batter or a baserunner is safe or out anywhere near home plate. Nothing better protects the chief umpire from being hit by pitches than a good catcher, and umpires tend to rely on this fact— which is why many go into a semi-crouch behind the catcher during pitches.

The four umpires comprise an umpire "crew" which stays together throughout the season. The umpire crews work both AL and NL games. MLB teams generally play a three or four-game series against one another, before moving on to play the next series against the next opponent. An umpire crew will call all of the games in the series, and then will move on to another city to call a series between other teams—the idea being that one umpire crew won't call back-to-back series involving the same baseball teams. The four umpires will switch around for each game, so that the umpire behind home plate may become the third base umpire for the next game, and the second base umpire for the game after that. If an umpire is injured and unable to continue, the game goes on with three umpires; if, as most often is the case (because he is hit by a foul ball) the injured man is the home plate umpire, one of the umpires out in the field will take his place. During the MLB playoffs, two outfield umpires are added for each game.

MLB umpires are the best in the world at what they do. All of these men went to umpire school and spent years in the minor leagues before coming up to the major leagues, so they really know their craft. When there is lightning-fast action out on the field, an umpire making a split-second decision is bound to make the occasional mistake; however, far more often, you will find that they get the call right. You will know this when you see the replay, either on the huge screen at the stadium, or on your television at home. More than once,

I have watched something happen during a game, and I was sure that the umpire made an incorrect call—only to realize when I watched the replay that he was right and I was wrong.

Every home plate umpire interprets the strike zone differently. Some umpires call a very tight strike zone, and a control pitcher who nibbles around the corners of the plate with his pitches will likely get more called balls than strikes. Other umpires call a wider strike zone, and pitchers will get pitches called as strikes that may appear to the spectator to be balls. The players know the umpires and their tendencies, and they adjust their pitching and their batting to comport with the way the game will be called. Sometimes pitchers, batters, and managers get upset at the way a home plate umpire is calling a game. However, I've actually seen batters turn to an umpire and respectfully inquire about how far a pitch they had let go by was outside of the strike zone. It is inevitable that there will be a tension between how a ballplayer or manager sees a play, and how an umpire sees it. Nonetheless, it is obvious that, overall, the players, manager, and coaches genuinely hold the MLB umpires in high regard.

Chapter 8

The Game

Over the past seven chapters, I have given you an overview and some observations about major league baseball. Now, let's go to a big league ballgame and put this information into context from a fan's-eye view.

Before the Game

The baseball game we are going to see is in Portland, Oregon, at the home stadium of the Portland Woodchucks (affectionately known to Woodchucks fans as "The Burrow"). The Charlotte Grits, from North Carolina, is the visiting team. It's a Saturday afternoon game, more likely to be crowded than a mid-week game. This is the first game of a three-game series between the two teams. Both the Woodchucks and the Grits are in the National League, so there is no designated hitter. It is late in the season, with only five games remaining on the schedule. Both teams are fighting to make the playoffs, and every win counts.

Oh, by the way, our tickets. We purchased our tickets online in advance since this would be an important game on a weekend. However, we could have purchased them at the stadium in person, or by telephone. Almost everyone has been to some public event at a stadium, arena, or theater, so we know the drill. First, we go through the turnstiles and have our bags examined and our tickets taken, with the stubs returned to us. We keep the ticket stubs readily available since they have our seat location information. We may also wish to hang onto the stubs as keepsakes, since we never know if the game will be memorable. [6]

Once we are inside the stadium, we follow the signs to our seating area. We will see the ushers near the entranceways to the seating areas (upper deck, lower deck, loge, ground level, outfield pavilions, bleachers etc.) available to guide us to our seats. We arrived early so that we could more easily find our seats (we are in the loge area, above and behind home plate, which gives us a good view of the entire ball field), and in order to get ballpark food before the game starts and the lines at the concession stands start to build. But more importantly, we can now watch the players take batting practice, or we may wander down near the bullpen to watch the starting pitchers warm up. Around the stadium, we see the seats beginning to fill up, and we see vendors walking around hawking snow cones, nachos, hotdogs, popcorn, candy, cotton candy, peanuts, soda, bottled water, and beer (basically, the same stuff available at the concession stands). Meanwhile out on the field, we see the players running, stretching, and catching (or as it's called, "shagging") fly balls.

---

[6] In September 1998, I had a chance to buy tickets to a Saturday game at Camden Yards, home of the Orioles baseball club, in Baltimore, Maryland. I went on Friday evening instead. If I had gone to the Saturday game, I would have been there for the final game of the longest streak of consecutive MLB games played in by any player . . . ever. The player who holds this record, Cal Ripken, Jr., chose to sit out the Sunday night game after having played in 2,632 straight games. Now **THAT** is a ticket stub I would have treasured as a keepsake.

Some of the pre-game crowd prefer to watch the power hitters take batting practice. We see others hanging near the outfield wall, calling out to the players who are shagging fly balls in the hope that they will toss the fans watching a caught baseball. I prefer to get as close as possible to one of the bullpens, so that I can watch the starting pitcher warm up before the game. One of baseball's small pleasures is watching a pitcher warming up in the dappled sunlight of a late summer's afternoon. There is nothing quite like hearing the smack of a baseball hitting the leather of a catcher's mitt in an almost empty stadium, while watching the small cloud of dust that rises from his mitt with each catch.

We head back to our seats. Looking around, we see several signs: mostly advertisements, many electronic, some important. Before the game starts, we locate the signs, or boards, that will have important information about the game and about what else is going on around Major League Baseball. Every stadium has informational boards, but they are in different places in different stadiums. The most important sign of all is the scoreboard. In the Woodchucks stadium, there is a large scoreboard out past the outfield seating, between left field and center field, that tells what is happening in the game. Once upon a time before today's technology, the scoreboard was updated by hand; and even though most are updated electronically these days, a few of the older parks still maintain the old tradition. Remember the Green Monster located at the edge of left field in Boston's Fenway Park? Well, built into that big ugly green wall is a scoreboard that is hand-operated by a fellow in a room just behind the wall.

We look at the scoreboard:

WOODCHUCKS
STADIUM

	1	2	3	4	5	6	7	8	9	10	R	H	E
GRITS													
WOODCHUCKS													

AT BAT   BALL   STRIKE   OUT

A Casual Fan's Guide

On the left of the scoreboard we see the name of the visiting team, Grits, with the name of the home team, Woodchucks, immediately below. Just to the right of the team names, we see a horizontal line of nine boxes for each team, left to right, one for each regular inning (plus one more box per team should the game go to extra innings). When a team scores a run, it will be reflected in the box for that inning. As the visiting team, the Grits will bat first, in the top of the inning, so it makes sense to put their name and row of boxes on top. To the right of those two rows of boxes is a line of three more boxes for each team. Above these boxes, are the letters "R" (for Runs), "H" (for Hits), and "E" (for Errors: when a defensive player drops the ball or overthrows it, and the baserunner advances to the next base) above the boxes.

After we locate the scoreboard, we look around to see where the other informational boards are in the Burrow, and what they show. It helps to become familiar with their location before the game starts; the information on them will be updated constantly as the game progresses. There will be boards showing the names and numbers of the defensive position players, the names and numbers of the pitchers (and sometimes their win-loss records, and ERAs), and the name and number of the batter and his batting average. The count of balls and strikes against the current batter may be shown on the scoreboard, or it may be shown on a separate board. There will be a separate board showing all of the teams around the country that are playing today, and which team won. Finally, there is an electronic board at the Burrow showing the speed of the pitch just thrown, and what type of pitch it was. A visiting team's fans may be skeptical about the speed; it is in the home team's interest to make visiting hitters think the pitches are coming faster than they really are.

After both teams have warmed up, the grounds crew comes back out onto the field to spray some water on the dirt part of the infield to keep the dust down, and make other final preparations. While we are on the subject of ball field maintenance and watering down the infield, know that a wet infield will slow down the baserunners. Consequently, if a visiting team has a lot of speedy baserunners and the home team doesn't, don't be surprised to see a soggy infield and a lot of muddy uniforms. If a team with good hitters is visiting, it is not unknown for a grounds crew to let the grass grow a bit longer on the ball field, since the longer grass will slow the speed of a hit ground ball. We see that the Burrow's infield is not soggy, but from the stands, we can't tell anything about the length of the grass.

Next, we see the opposing managers meet with the home plate umpire at home plate and exchange batting lineups. Here is the Grits' batting order:

1. Shortstop
2. Second Baseman
3. Catcher
4. First Baseman
5. Third Baseman
6. Center Fielder
7. Right Fielder
8. Left Fielder
9. Pitcher

The batting order for the Woodchucks is somewhat different:

1. Second Baseman
2. Shortstop
3. First Baseman
4. Left Fielder
5. Center Fielder
6. Catcher
7. Right Fielder
8. Third Baseman
9. Pitcher

After the exchange of batting lineup cards, the two teams line up along the foul lines in front of their respective dugouts, remove their caps, and face the American flag flying high above the outfield wall. The stadium announcer calls out over the loudspeakers asking everyone to rise for our national anthem, we do so, and listen while a local country-western singer gives her rendition of the Star Spangled Banner.

At the conclusion, we hear a roar from the crowd, and see a scurrying around on the ball field as players and umpires move to take up their positions as we sit down. The Woodchucks pitcher throws a few warm-up pitches, the infielders toss around a few warm-up throws to each other, and everyone is ready to go. The first Grits batter walks up to the plate, gripping and swinging his bat, perhaps visualizing the hit he hopes to make. The home plate umpire calls out "Play Ball!"

A Heads-Up

You would not want to read a pitch-by-pitch account of an entire baseball game, and such a layout would defeat the purpose that I am trying to accomplish with this book. However, I do think it will be helpful to go through the first inning of the game in some detail, describing what you are seeing and why it is happening. After the first inning, the description will be less detailed. My aim here is to expose you to a selection of things that you might see if you go to a ballgame, so that when one occurs you won't be sitting there wondering, "What just happened?" I have tried to pack a lot of action into these nine innings, and you should realize that it is extremely unlikely that you will see all of the events I am about to describe in one game. Anyway, the home plate umpire has spoken, so let's get to it and see what happens next.

The Early Innings

First Inning

Top of the First

The Grits shortstop is their lead-off batter. He steps into the batter's box and hoists his bat, preparing to receive the first pitch. Meanwhile, the Grits second baseman is in the batter's circle (also known as the on-deck circle), taking practice swings or "cuts" at an imaginary baseball with his bat, and readying himself to step up to the plate at a moment's notice. Sometimes players slide a metal "donut" over the bat handle and down onto the barrel to add some weight for practice swings in the on-deck circle; this makes the bat feel lighter after they take it off and swing at a live pitch.

As the shortstop comes to bat, the public address announcer introduces him. Different announcers have different styles. One notable announcer, Bob Sheppard, announced Yankee games from 1951 until he retired in 2007. He announced every batter the same way, intoning in an elegant voice, "Now batting," and then the player's position, his uniform number, his name, and his uniform number again. For example, if Joe Smith was the Grits shortstop, and his uniform number was 4, Bob Sheppard would introduce him thusly: "Now batting, shortstop, number 4, Joe Smith, number 4." It's not so much what he said, but rather his stylish simplicity that caught your attention. We listen as the Woodchucks announcer introduces the first Grits batter.

The pitcher goes into his wind-up and throws a high inside fastball, up close to the batter's chest, because he thinks the batter is "crowding the plate" to gain an edge, and he wants to "brush him back." The batter takes the pitch without swinging, and the umpire bellows out "Strike!" as he signals the call by pointing at the batter with his left hand and raising the traditional clenched right fist. An umpire always calls a strike using his right arm, and some do it by flinging their right hand off to the side with an outstretched forefinger.

On the second pitch, a curveball, the batter swings and misses; again the umpire calls out "Strike!" and raises a clenched fist. Then the umpire signals the count, holding up two fingers of his right hand. The next pitch is a breaking ball down in the dirt that the pitcher hopes the batter will "chase;" the umpire signals it as a ball by raising one finger on his left hand, and shows the count by holding up the two fingers on his right hand; in other words, the count is 1 and 2 (remember, balls are always called out first). Some umpires only signal strikes, so if you don't see any signal, the pitch was a ball.

Sitting up in the stands, we see the umpire's larger movements with his arms or body, but it is difficult for us to see his fingers and hands, or to hear him call out. Not to worry; the pitch count is shown on electronic boards conveniently located around the stadium. If we were watching the game on television, we would see the count displayed on the screen.

The Woodchucks pitcher throws the fourth pitch straight down the pipe at around 94 miles per hour. The Grits batter gets wood on it and lines a ground ball into the gap between the shortstop and the second baseman, out into right center field. The center fielder, knowing that the leadoff batter is a slap hitter who is unlikely to hit the ball far, had already moved up to about midway between the outfield wall and the edge of the infield. He runs forward to meet the ball, scoops it up with his glove, and transfers it to his throwing hand as he looks toward first base. Simultaneously, the first baseman has moved to the base and is touching it with his foot, waiting for a possible throw from the center fielder. In addition, the pitcher has sprinted off the pitcher's mound to a place between the foul line and the right field wall, getting behind and backing up the first baseman, positioning himself to field the ball in case of an errant throw by the center fielder.

Meanwhile, the batter, who became a baserunner as soon as he hit the ball, flings his bat off to the side of the infield as he takes off running toward first base, reaches, and then rounds the bag when he gets there. We see him come to a screeching halt when he hears his first base coach calling for him to hold on first. He sees that the center fielder has cleanly fielded the baseball and is ready to throw to either the first baseman or the second baseman as necessary, so he quickly steps back onto the first base bag. The leadoff batter for the Grits is safely on base with a single.

Once the baserunner is safe on first base, the next Grits batter moves into the batter's box, and the Woodchucks pitcher turns his attention to him. The pitcher sets, he throws—and the batter hits a "flare" that goes just over the head of the shortstop and lands in the outfield. By the time the Woodchucks left fielder moves up and collects the ball, there are Grits baserunners safely on first and second base.

The Grits third batter comes to the plate. Because the Woodchucks pitcher has two men on base, with no outs, he is concerned. He knows that this player is a power hitter, and he doesn't want to give him a good pitch to knock out of the ballpark, causing three runs to score. From experience, the batter knows what is going on in the pitcher's mind, and he decides to wait for a good pitch that he can hit. Also, we can see that the Grits manager is signaling through the third base coach what he wants the batter to do: whether he wants the batter to swing away, to bunt, or to take a pitch. Of course we don't know what the signals mean, but in this situation (two men on base, no outs, and early in the game), the manager would be signaling the Grits' batter to "hit away," meaning the batter can swing at his discretion with everything he's got. Separately, you will notice that before each pitch, the two men on base move a few feet in the direction of the next base (it's called "leading off," or "taking a lead off of" the base), just in case the batter hits a ground ball and they have to hightail it to the next base. If the batter doesn't swing at a pitch during his at-bat, they return to their respective bases each time the catcher throws the ball back to the pitcher.

The first two pitches to this Grits batter are intentional balls—really bad pitches that are unhittable (known as "waste" pitches); the batter doesn't swing, but instead continues to wait patiently for something decent to hit. At this point, the batter doesn't know if the pitcher is going to throw another intentional ball, or something over the plate that is hittable, so the batter continues to wait. The third pitch is a sinker for a called strike. The next pitch, a curveball, is just off the outside of the plate, and the batter still holds back. The fifth pitch is a breaking ball down in the dirt. The batter was expecting a low fastball, and he swings at the pitch and misses. Now, the count is sitting at 3-2, or three balls and two strikes; this is known as a "full count" because, unless the batter fouls off the next pitch, he will either hit the ball, strike out, or earn a walk to first base.

The pitcher sets and throws the ball—and the hitter hits a ground ball that is collected (swept up) by the shortstop. The Grits runners on first and second are moving as soon as they see the hit is a grounder—the baserunner on first base has to make room for the baserunner who just hit the ball, and the baserunner on second has to make room for the baserunner coming from first base. These two players already had a substantial lead off their bases, and they fly down the basepaths, making tracks for the next base. The Woodchucks shortstop glances toward third base, but the baserunner from second is almost there already and the shortstop isn't sure he can make the play. Instead, the shortstop flips the ball to the second baseman, who touches the second base bag with his toe (he can touch it with any part of his body or even his glove) before the runner from first can get there, forcing the runner out. The Woodchucks second baseman then spins and fires the baseball to the first baseman, over the oncoming runner that is sliding into second base with the intention of disrupting the throw. Before the hitter-turned-baserunner can make it to first base, the first baseman catches the baseball with one foot touching the bag, forcing the runner out.

The umpires behind first base and second base are watching all this intently, eyes focused on what is going on immediately in front of them. Once they see the defending players touch the two bases while in possession of the baseball, before the baserunners arrive, they yell "Out!" while jerking their clenched fists up and down in a hammering motion. What we just saw was a double play, and since we are at the Woodchucks stadium, we hear the roar of approval from the crowd.

However, the pitcher is not out of the woods quite yet. There are only two outs, and the runner on third base is a threat to score. Moreover, the Grits' best hitter (remember, the fourth batter is the heart of the batting lineup) is coming to the plate. To make matters worse, this particular batter has a history of hitting well against the Woodchucks pitcher. However, the Woodchucks catcher is familiar with the batter as well, and knows that the batter has a tough time "laying off" sinker balls. He signals for the pitcher to throw such a breaking ball, but the pitcher shakes him off. He wants to "set the batter up" with a couple of pitches high in the strike zone before he throws that pitch.

The first pitch is high and outside—a ball. The pitcher decides he wants to disrupt the timing of the batter so that he is not expecting a pitch at regular intervals. The pitcher calls for time (a brief time-out), ambles down to the back edge of the mound, and bends down to retie a shoelace. Stepping back up to the top of the mound, the pitcher kicks the toes of his shoes a couple of times on the edge of the pitching rubber as if to knock off dirt that has collected between the cleats. He adjusts his cap, and then steps up onto the rubber. He sets, looks over or "checks" the runner on third base to make sure he stays near the bag, and throws a high inside pitch that brushes the batter back from the plate.

As soon as the catcher throws the ball back to the pitcher, he sets and prepares to throw another pitch. Batters are given a fair amount of time to ready themselves between pitches, but as soon as the pitcher sees that the Grits batter is ready, the Woodchucks pitcher throws a sinker. The batter takes the bait; he swings, but does not connect solidly with the baseball, hitting a hard, fast-moving grounder into the waiting glove of the Woodchucks' shortstop. The shortstop holds the ball just long enough to glance at the runner on third base—"freezing" him there—before throwing it to his first baseman. The throw is high, but the first baseman hops into the air, catches it, and lands with one foot touching the base just before the runner arrives, forcing him out. So ends the top half of the inning.

Why didn't the Woodchucks shortstop throw the ball to his third baseman to try and get the Grits baserunner out, or to the catcher to keep the baserunner from scoring? He didn't need to. There were already two outs, and one more out would have ended the Grits' "at-bat." So long as the shortstop got the ball to first base for the put-out before the baserunner on third base could score, the throw to first base would force the third out; and it was the only sure play, since the baserunner on third base likely would have "held" on the bag. In that scenario, a throw to the third baseman would have resulted in the batter being safe on first, the baserunner being safe on third, and another Grits batter coming up to bat.

Bottom of the First

Now it is the Grits' turn to take the field and the Woodchucks' turn to bat. The first batter in the Woodchucks lineup is the second baseman. He is not a particularly strong batter, but he is fast at running the bases, and he has lightning-quick reflexes. He bunts, and the ball slowly dribbles out into the infield, midway between third base and the pitcher's mound. The Grits third baseman was playing too far back, and the pitcher is slow to react. The third baseman gets to the slowly rolling ball and fields it on the run, leaps, twists, and throws the baseball to the first baseman in one long smooth motion—but he's too late! The speedy baserunner is flying down the basepath, and is almost to first base even before the ball leaves the third baseman's hand. At full speed, his foot touches the base just before the ball slaps into the first baseman's mitt. As the baserunner gallops past the first base umpire, slows, and turns to his right to trot back to first base, the umpire spreads his arms out to his sides signaling that the runner is safe.

Once upon a time, baserunners could not overrun any of the bases. So long as they were off a base, they could be tagged out. However, that rule was changed long ago, because it gave the defense too great an advantage (there is no way that the Woodchucks lead-off batter could have made it to first base safely if he had had to decelerate before reaching the bag). In the modern era, it is okay for a baserunner to overrun first base, so long as he turns to his right—in the direction of foul territory—before he returns to the base. It is not okay for the baserunner to turn to his left when

115

returning to first base. Why not? Because if he did so, the first base umpire could rule that he was trying to get to second base, and it would be okay for the first baseman to tag him out.

Now we have the Woodchucks' leadoff hitter on first base, and the second batter in the Woodchucks lineup is at the plate. He hits a fly ball into the gap between the Grits left fielder and center fielder, and both defensive players race to get to the baseball. Some fly balls are high and soft, meaning that they seem to stay up in the air forever; some are powerful "moon shots," meaning that they leave the ball field—and sometimes the ballpark— like a launched rocket headed to the moon; and some are more like line drives through the air, barely rising as they head into the outfield. The batter really smacked this ball forcefully, but it did not go up and off like a roman candle. Instead, the ball flew long, straight, and fast; hit once on the hard-packed dirt of the outfield track out in left centerfield, and bounced over the outfield wall, which was not very high at that particular spot. Since the baseball hit the ground before it went over the outfield wall, it is what is known as a "ground-rule double," meaning that the batter gets to go to second base, and the base runner in front of him gets to advance two bases; here, to third base. If the preceding baserunner had been on second base instead of first base, he would have been allowed to go home, thus scoring a run.

The Woodchucks now have men on second and third base, with no one out, and their third batter comes to the plate. He hits a grounder into left field, but the left fielder has come up close to the infield and he fields the ball quickly—so quickly in fact that the Woodchucks third base coach holds the runner at third. There are now baserunners on every base (in baseball terminology, "the bases are loaded") and no one is out.

The Grits pitcher knows that if he gives up any kind of a hit or a walk, someone will score. When the fourth Woodchucks batter (the cleanup man) comes to the plate, the pitcher slows down and becomes cautious—too cautious. With no outs and the bases loaded, the batter has the green light from his manager to swing away, and the pitcher knows this too. His first two pitches are waste pitches; breaking balls down in the dirt that are obvious balls. The next two pitches nibble on the outside edges of the plate, but the batter isn't biting, and the umpire calls them balls. Because this batter has excellent plate discipline and refused to take the bait, he earns a walk to first base. Since the bases were loaded, the runner on third base walks into home to score a run. The Woodchucks are now ahead 1-0, and still there are no outs in the bottom of the first inning. The Woodchucks fans know that the Grits pitcher is rattled because he walked in a run, and they begin to taunt him loudly.

The Woodchucks center fielder bats next. He pops the ball high up into the infield. While the ball is still in the air, the home plate umpire throws his right hand into the air and yells "Infield Fly!" This means that the batter (and only the batter) has been ruled out. The infield fly rule came into being in the late 19th century to prohibit a defensive player (here, a Grits player) from intentionally allowing a ball to drop to the ground, and then picking it up and getting multiple baserunners out. It is a rule that—generally—operates to the advantage of the team at bat, even though it means an out for that team.

The infield fly rule applies only in very limited circumstances: (1) there must be baserunners on at least first and second base; (2) the ball was not bunted (even if it pops up when it is bunted, because a bunted ball is intended to land in the infield); (3) the hit ball was not a line drive (which might well go through the infield); and (4) there is, at most, only one out—if the team at bat has two outs, then a called third out would defeat the purpose of the rule.

The sixth man in the Woodchucks' lineup is their catcher. The Grits pitcher runs the count against him up to 2-2 (two balls and two strikes). Then, out of the corner of his eye, the pitcher notices that during this at-bat, the baserunner at third base has moved off the bag, inching farther and farther down the basepath toward home plate. Remember, the pitcher was getting a bit unsettled when the bases were loaded with nobody out. He walks off the mound, picks up the rosin bag, shakes it to get some of the sticky stuff on his throwing fingers, and then slowly steps back up to the rubber. The pitcher takes his ballcap off and wipes his forehead with his right forearm, ostensibly to remove the sweat—but it's actually a signal. The next throw is what is known as a "pitchout," where the pitcher throws the ball high and outside, away from the batter. When the thrown ball leaves the pitcher's hand, the catcher steps out of the catcher's box and away from the batter, catches the thrown ball cleanly, and fires it to the waiting third baseman. The baserunner is caught flatfooted. He turns and tries to make it back to third base but he is too late, and the third baseman tags him out; he has been picked off. The third base umpire pumps his right fist and makes the call: "Out!" Two away.

The Grits pitcher now has a full count (3-2) on the Woodchucks batter, and the pitcher throws him a ball and walks him. Once again, the bases are loaded, and the Woodchucks first baseman is now the baserunner on third. The pitcher realizes that he needs to concentrate on getting the next batter out (the Grits right fielder, batting seventh in the order) so that another run isn't scored. Nonetheless, he makes an errant throw that glances off the tip of the outstretched mitt of the catcher and bounces all the way to the screened barrier (called a "backstop") far to his rear. The catcher rises and turns, ripping off his mask so that he can see where the ball went. While he chases down what is known officially as a "wild pitch," the baserunner on third seizes his chance and hightails it for home. As soon as the pitcher sees that he has overthrown the catcher, he dashes to cover home plate should the catcher retrieve the ball in time. Alas, it's too late! The baserunner storms across home plate to score another run. The Woodchucks lead the Grits 2-0, and with two outs, still have runners on first and second base.

The Grits pitcher is frustrated. The Woodchucks batter at the plate had backed out of the way so as not to interfere when his teammate on third base was heading for home. Now, when he steps up to the plate to continue his at-bat, the pitcher rears back and fires an inside fastball, meant to be high and inside. However, the ball sails in on the batter, and before he can jerk away from the plate, he is hit in the forearm. The home plate umpire directs the hit batter to first base. The umpire then steps into the infield to warn the pitcher that if he hits another batter he will be thrown out of the game. Although the warning is directed at the Grits pitcher, it is also meant to serve notice on the Woodchucks that their pitcher should not retaliate or he too will be tossed out. The bases are loaded again.

As I told you back in Chapter Five, intimidation is one of the tools that a pitcher uses to get batters out. Here, the pitcher knows that, regardless of the umpire's warning, the next Woodchucks batter will be thinking about getting hit by a baseball, and that will affect how the batter reacts to what the pitcher throws. Also, while we are on the subject of hit batters, be aware that the baseball doesn't actually have to hit the batter's body; it is not unusual for batters to be awarded first base when the ball merely brushes the fronts of their jerseys or their pants legs. Too, a key element is whether the batter tried to get out of the way of the oncoming baseball if he had time to do so. If the umpire believes that the batter could have moved out of the way and avoided being hit, then he will not be awarded first base.

Again, the bases are loaded, and the Woodchucks third baseman steps up to the plate. The Grits pitcher knows that this Woodchucks batter is a weak hitter, and sure enough, the pitcher gets him to swing at three mediocre pitches in succession. The first inning ends with the Woodchucks holding a 2-0 lead. They left three men on base, so the Grits are thankful to get out of the inning only two runs down; it could have been much worse. At the end of one, the Grits have 0 runs, 2 hits, and 0 errors, and the Woodchucks have 2 runs, 3 hits, and 0 errors.

Baseball players can be a superstitious lot. Keep your eyes on the pitcher as he walks toward the Grits dugout and see if he hops over the foul line. For some reason, a lot of pitchers do. Why? No rational reason that I've ever heard.

Second Inning

Top of the Second

Although the Woodchucks went through the first eight batters in their lineup in the bottom of the first inning, only four of the Grits came up to the plate in their first turn at bat. We start the second inning with the fifth batter in their lineup, the third baseman. He strikes out.

The next batter gets a single, as does the batter after him; so now we have two men on base with one out. The Grits left fielder hits a line drive directly to the shortstop, who catches it cleanly. As an announcer calling the game would say, "Two on, two out, and the pitcher (the announcer will identify him by name) is coming up to bat." The Grits pitcher strikes out to end the top of the second inning, stranding two men on base. Meanwhile, the sky has grown progressively grayer, and a light mist has started to fall.

Bottom of the Second

The first batter (the Woodchucks pitcher) appears to strike out—but wait. On the third strike, the Grits catcher doesn't catch the ball cleanly, and the ball goes dribbling away from him. Had he caught the ball the batter would have been out. However, since the catcher did not catch the ball, the batter is not out. He can run to first base as if he had hit the ball—and it is up to the catcher to either tag him out or throw the ball to first base to make the put-out. To avoid any confusion, you should know that the key event here is that the catcher did not catch the baseball on what would have been the third strike. Consequently, even if (1) the pitch had been a called third strike, or (2) if the batter had swung at the pitch and completely missed it, he could have run to first base as if he had hit the ball.

We see the batter take off running as the catcher retrieves the baseball and turns toward first base. By this time, the baserunner is already over halfway to first base, so the catcher fires the ball in the direction of the waiting first baseman. However, in his haste, the catcher overthrows the ball and it goes sailing off down along the right field foul line. The right fielder, as he is trained to do, has moved over to back up the first baseman in case this should happen. Nonetheless, by the time the right fielder gets to the ball and collects it, the baserunner has safely reached second base. The Grits catcher is having a bad time of it; first, he is charged with a "passed ball" for missing what should have been an easy catch for the out, and then he is charged with an error for over-throwing the baseball to the first baseman.

Who decides that the Grits catcher would be charged with a passed ball and an error? The official scorer does. Stepping back from our ballgame, let me give you some general background about the official scorer (sometimes informally called the "scorekeeper"). Major League Baseball designates an official scorer for every ballgame, and it is his job to make the official record of the game. He records all runs, hits, and errors, and makes certain judgment calls, including whether something is an error, whether a catcher should be charged with a passed ball, or whether a pitcher has made a wild pitch.[7] For instance, if a defensive player doesn't make a catch, it might be deemed an error, or not, depending on whether the official scorer thought the ball was catchable. Similarly, a pitch that the catcher doesn't catch might be recorded as a passed ball (and charged to the catcher), or it might be recorded as a wild pitch, meaning it is uncatchable (and therefore charged to the pitcher).

---

[7] Don't get confused with what the umpires do and what the official scorer does; their roles are completely different. The umpires actively call the game out on the field as the game proceeds, while the official scorer records the game, including the calls that the umpires make.

One more thing before we head back to our game: here is an interesting tweak to the scenario I've just described. Let's say the pitcher had struck out the first two batters he faced in the inning, and then he struck out this batter, but the catcher didn't catch the ball, and this batter/baserunner made it safely to first base. In this situation, the official scorer will credit the pitcher with having struck out three batters. If the pitcher then strikes out another batter, he will be credited with having struck out four batters in a half-inning. I find this to be one of the odd little rules of baseball that comes up only once in a blue moon, and in all of the games I have been to or watched on television, I have never seen it happen—but we should be aware of the possibility that it could. Turning back to our game, we see the error posted on the stadium scoreboard.

The next Woodchucks batter, the second baseman, hits a ground ball up the gap between first base and second base. The runner on second base had a nice lead off the bag, and he takes off running just as soon as he sees the ball bounce through the infield. As he heads into third base, the third base coach is screaming at the baserunner to keep going; we can't hear the third base coach, but we can see him jumping up and down and waving the baserunner home with a large looping windmill motion. We watch as the runner rounds third base and heads for home. Meanwhile, the Grits right fielder has secured the baseball and sees what is happening. This right fielder has a "cannon" for an arm. In what appears to be an almost effortless motion, he cocks and fires the ball toward home plate. The ball sails over the heads of the infielders, bounces once in the infield, and smacks into the waiting mitt of the catcher.

The Grits catcher is down on his left knee, which is planted just to the left of home plate. His right leg is stretched out behind him and angled to his right, so that he is directly over and covering home plate with his body, physically blocking the baserunner from reaching the plate. He fields the baseball with both hands, no more than half a second before the baserunner plows into him, knocking him over and backwards. If the catcher drops the ball, the baserunner will have scored a run; if he doesn't drop the ball, then the baserunner is out. After what seems like forever—but really isn't—we see the catcher come up off the ground holding the ball in his throwing hand, held high, leaving no doubt that he has retained possession. The umpire jerks his right arm up and back as he calls the Woodchucks baserunner out.

Remember that Woodchucks baserunner who just hit the ball? While the Grits right fielder was collecting the baseball and throwing it home, the runner took second base standing up. He, we, and everyone else in the stadium have been watching the action at home plate. The baserunner keeps moving, sliding off the bag toward third, thinking that he might try to stretch his double into a triple. Bad idea, or as I like to say, his mind is writing a check that his body can't cash. As the Grits catcher comes up holding the baseball, he sees the Woodchucks baserunner between second and third, and fires it to the second baseman. The Grits second baseman catches the ball and moves off second toward the runner. Meanwhile, the third baseman has come off his bag, positioning himself between third base and the baserunner. The Woodchucks baserunner makes a move toward third, but the second baseman flips the baseball to the Grits shortstop, who moves toward the runner with the ball in his throwing hand. The baserunner turns back in the direction of second base, but the Grits shortstop is quicker and tags him out. This defensive play is called a "rundown," or a "pickle" (as, the baserunner is in a pickle), and the second out in the bottom of the second inning has been recorded.

The next Woodchucks batter comes up to hit, and knocks a gentle grounder to the first baseman, just inside the foul line. The first baseman fields it cleanly, and steps on the base to end the inning. As the opposing teams change places, the home plate umpire steps forward to sweep off home plate, as we will see him do every once in a while throughout the game. At the bottom of the second inning, the Grits have 0 runs, 4 hits, and 1 error, and the Woodchucks have 2 runs, 3 hits, and 0 errors.

Third Inning

Top of the Third

We've seen the Grits go through their entire batting order, and now they start through again. The Grits first batter of the inning (the shortstop) does his job—he gets on base by earning a walk. However, the Grits' second batter strikes out. Nonetheless, the Grits' players have been paying attention, watching the Woodchucks pitcher work and seeing what kind of "stuff" he has today. Now, they begin to get to him.

The next batter up hits a double. The batter after him also hits a double, driving the two baserunners in front of him home. At last, the Grits are "on the board" with two runs and with a runner on second base. Then, lightning strikes—the fifth Grits batter up in the inning hits a home run. Suddenly, the Grits are leading 4 to 2.

At this point, the Woodchucks pitcher is reeling. All he wants is to get out of the inning without giving up any more runs, but there is no relief in sight. The next batter is the sixth batter in the Grits lineup, the center fielder. This batter is not noted for being much of a power hitter, but he too hauls off and wallops a towering home run. "Enough of this," says the Woodchucks pitcher to himself. When the next batter comes to the plate, he rears back and fires the ball straight at the batter. The batter tries to back away from the oncoming ball, but it hits him in the ribcage and he drops to his knees. As a loud chorus of boos pours from the stands, the home plate umpire quickly steps forward between the batter and the pitcher and ejects the pitcher from the game.

We watch as the Grits erupt from their dugout like an army of fire ants, headed directly toward the pitcher's mound. The Woodchucks immediately follow suit. The players, and most of the coaches, meet in the middle of the infield, and shouting, pushing, and shoving promptly commences. Baseball is not like professional ice hockey; in other words, one rarely sees professional baseball players go after each other with no holds barred; when there is a baseball brawl, it's likely going to look more like a bunch of grown men wearing pajamas engaging in a pillow fight. The pitchers out in the opposing bullpens make a half-hearted jog up to the scene of the action, but they don't do more than loiter around just outside the main mass of players. About the last thing a major league pitcher wants is to get involved in an on-field melee, which could result in a career-ending injury to his throwing hand. In our game here, calmer heads prevail soon enough, the umpires order everyone back to their dugouts, and things settle down.

After the batter is checked out to make sure he's okay (he is, but he'll be sore later), he proceeds to first base. When everyone has returned to where they are supposed to be, play resumes. While the two teams were out on the ball field posturing and acting silly, the Woodchucks replacement pitcher has continued to warm up in the bullpen with a bullpen catcher the team carries on its payroll solely for that purpose. Consequently, when play resumes, he's largely ready to go. The next batter hits a ground ball to the Woodchucks shortstop, who flips the ball to his second baseman, who steps on the bag and then hurls the ball to first base, making a double play to end the inning. Doesn't quite seem fair to the player who was hit by the pitch, but these things seem to have a way of balancing out.

Remember that we are in Portland, and that it rains a fair amount in the Pacific Northwest. The light mist that started to come down in the middle of the second inning turns into a steady drizzle just about the time of the on-field contretemps. Now the rain is pouring down in earnest, and the home plate umpire calls a rain delay.

The players are lucky; they get to sit out the rain in the dugout, or go back into the dressing room for a snack and a drink. The fans generally head back into the covered areas of the stadium and wait it out, or if that's not possible, they drape something over their heads and accept that it's going to be a bad hair day. Meanwhile, the grounds crew rushes out to unroll a tarp and drag it over the infield; you'll be surprised at how quickly they can do this, even though a tarp can weigh as much as 1,500 pounds. The outfield will get wet, but most of the game action is in the infield, where the dirt surface could quickly turn to mud.

This is a good time to talk with your friends or catch up with folks on your cell phone, take a walk around and get some snacks, or watch the programming on the monitors scattered throughout the stadium. Otherwise . . . you wait. If, after thirty minutes, the rain doesn't stop or it doesn't look like it is going to stop, the home plate umpire can call the game over.

If he does, and five innings haven't been played, the game will be rescheduled. You'll get a ticket to come back to the stadium at some point later in the season and see a do-over of the game from the beginning. However, if at least five innings have been played and the home plate umpire calls the game, then the team that is on top at that point is declared the winner—except in the playoffs, or if the game is in the middle of an inning and the visiting team has just jumped ahead. In those situations, the game is suspended, and when the game resumes (perhaps the next day, if scheduling and the weather permit) play picks up where things left off.

I once went to a ballgame in Baltimore to watch the Oakland Athletics play the Orioles at Camden Yards ballpark. As I recall, there were only two days remaining in the regular season. Although the Orioles were way back in the standings, the Athletics (often called the "A's") were in the playoff hunt. They needed a win to make it into the playoffs, and there would not have been enough time to reschedule and play the game again before the end of the season. Again, if memory serves, the game was close, and as I recall, it went for the full nine innings. This is the only baseball game I have ever attended where the last several innings were played at night in a downpour—with gusting wind; the temperature must have been down around 60 degrees in the later innings. The playing conditions were absolutely miserable, and when you have slick baseballs and a sopping wet ball field, the likelihood of players being injured rises. I am sure that the home plate umpire would have called the game under any other circumstances (after all, he and the rest of his crew were out there getting drenched and shivering along with the players), but it needed to be played. The point is that unusual games like this do sometimes happen.

However, today is our lucky day. After about ten minutes the rain starts to let up, and within another ten minutes the gray sky begins to lighten and the sun peeks through the clouds. A few minutes later, the grounds crew reappears to pull the tarp off the infield and to tidy up. If the rain delay had gone on much longer, the managers would have had to decide whether to replace their pitchers, because their arms might have stiffened up during the delay, increasing the possibility of injury. Fortunately, that's not a problem: the Woodchucks had to bring in a new pitcher anyway, and although he's been knocked around a bit, the Grits pitcher has only pitched two innings. After a few warmup pitches, he seems ready to go again.

Bottom of the Third

The first batter up is the Woodchucks first baseman. He hits a single on the first pitch. The second batter, the left fielder, hits a fly ball that lands between the center fielder and the right fielder, and bounces to the outfield wall. The baserunner at first base had been waiting close to the bag so that he could "tag up" if necessary. When he sees the ball hit the ground, he immediately takes off in a sprint; he rounds second and heads toward third. The right fielder beats the center fielder to the ball, snatches it up, and makes the throw to third base. The runner barely "beats out" the throw by sliding head first, right arm extended in front of him, hand reaching to touch the bag—always a dangerous move that can seriously injure a baserunner. Meanwhile, the batter, now baserunner, has rounded first base and is flying toward second as fast as he can motor. Upon receiving the baseball, the third baseman immediately fires it back to the second baseman, who has moved to straddle the bag. The baserunner has already committed, having passed the point where he could get safely back to first base. About six feet from the bag he throws himself into a controlled foot-first slide—the preferable technique for sliding into a bag. The second baseman catches the ball and swings his glove down in a windmill fashion, grazing the baserunner's foot—which the second baseman has physically blocked from touching the bag with his leg. One away, with a runner on third.

Before we move on, let me explain what I meant when, in the paragraph above, I said that the baserunner could tag up. When a runner is on base, he generally takes a lead off the base, perhaps ten or fifteen feet from the bag—whatever he thinks is the maximum distance he can be from the base and still get back if necessary to keep from being put out. The baserunner takes this lead so that he can have a head start getting to the next base if the batter hits a ground ball, or if the baserunner is thinking of stealing the next base. It is permissible under the rules of baseball for him to do this. However, if the batter hits a fly ball, the baserunner has to go back to the base and literally tag it with his toe after the ball is caught before he can take off to get to the next base. Why? Because otherwise he would have too great an advantage over the defenders when he is running from one base to the next.

The next batter up (the Woodchucks center fielder) walks. With one out, runners on first and third, and with the Grits holding a three-run lead, the manager of the Woodchucks decides to gamble. He knows that his player on third base, although not a speedster, is quick enough to steal an occasional base and has good judgment. Also, his baserunner on first can fly. Although we can't see him do it, the Woodchucks manager gives the sign to his base coaches for both players to steal when the right pitch comes along. What we do see is the baserunners taking good-sized leads off their respective bags and readying themselves. The next batter takes two balls and a strike. The fourth pitch is low and outside, the batter again does not swing, and the runner on first base takes off. The Grits catcher fires the ball to second base, and the second baseman catches it and makes the tag. As soon as the baseball has left the catcher's hand, we see the baserunner on third go into a full sprint for home. The second baseman throws quickly back to the catcher, but he's too late; the runner scores standing up. Two away, with a run in, and the score is now Grits 5, Woodchucks 3.

The batter is "sitting on a full count" (3-2), waiting for a sweet pitch straight down the pipe. He gets what he wants, but he doesn't get his bat squarely on the ball, and he grounds out to the Grits second baseman to end the inning—all in all, a rather anticlimactic finish to an action-packed third inning. At the end of three, the Grits have 5 runs, 8 hits, and 1 error, and the Woodchucks have 3 runs, 4 hits, and 0 errors.

The Middle Innings

Fourth Inning

Top of the Fourth

The leadoff hitter for the Grits is their pitcher. The Woodchucks' new pitcher immediately walks him; an inauspicious beginning, and never a good thing for the team playing defense—you would be surprised how often the leadoff runner in an inning scores when he gets on base. The next batter, the Grits shortstop, comes to the plate. However, the crowd can tell the pitcher is troubled about having the leadoff runner on first base because he repeatedly throws to the first baseman, intending (1) to pick the runner off, or (2) to hold him near the first base bag so that the runner doesn't take too big a lead. As an aside, if we were at the Grits home stadium and the Woodchucks pitcher did this, the Grits fans would boo him loudly each time he threw over to first. In any event, the Grits batter takes two strikes, and then hits a pop-up to the Woodchucks third baseman. One man on, and one away.

The following batter, the Grits second baseman, has a long at-bat: the first two pitches are balls, then a strike, then a "foul tip" (where the batter gets wood on the ball, but it "tips" sharply and directly into the catcher's mitt) for another strike, then three foul balls in succession that are not "playable" by the defense, and then another ball. Finally, the Woodchucks pitcher strikes the batter out. One on and two away.

The Grits catcher is up next. The Woodchucks pitcher steps up on the rubber and goes into his set (throwing position): he looks to first, looks in to home plate, and then looking back toward first, he shifts his grip on the ball nestled in his glove—and then, unconsciously and in a barely perceptible motion, he slides the ball out of the glove with his throwing hand and then slides it back in. The home plate umpire stops play, walks forward, points at the pitcher, and calls out "balk." He awards the batter first base, and he directs the baserunner on first base to second base. Now we have two men on base, and two away. The Grits first baseman now comes up to bat—and promptly strikes out to end the top of the inning. That sure lets the air out of the balloon, doesn't it? Perhaps you are gaining a sense that baseball games play out in unpredictable ways. This unpredictability is one of the things that makes baseball fun, and keeps fans coming back; you never know what you're going to see next.

Bottom of the Fourth

The bottom of the fourth inning goes fast. The Woodchucks right fielder leads off by striking out. The second batter, the Woodchucks third baseman, hits a double. Not unexpectedly, the Woodchucks pitcher also strikes out. Then, the Woodchucks shortstop hits a gentle ground ball to the Grits second baseman, who throws to the first baseman for an easy put-out to end the inning. This was a short half-inning, but they can be shorter. Sometimes, but not too often, a pitcher can get out of an inning having thrown only three or four good pitches. At the end of four, the Woodchucks left a baserunner stranded on second base, and the score is still 5-3.

Fifth Inning

Top of the Fifth

The first batter up is the Grits third baseman. On the second pitch, he slams a line drive, called a comebacker, right back to the pitcher—more accurately, right back at the pitcher's head.

The comebacker is among the most dangerous things that can happen in the game of baseball. Put yourself in the pitcher's place: He starts his windup, or set, from the pitching rubber, 60 feet, 6 inches from home plate. By the time he finishes his throwing motion and lands at the front of the pitcher's mound, the pitcher is—depending on his throwing motion—generally between 52 to 55 feet from home plate. At that point, the pitcher is still off-balance. His hands are dangling at his sides, and he is not wearing a helmet, facemask, or pads; in sum, he is completely defenseless. If he just threw a fastball, it was likely traveling somewhere above 90 miles per hour, and now it's coming straight back at him, giving him only hundredths of a second to react. Under these circumstances, and even if the pitcher has lightning-fast reflexes, he will be very fortunate to avoid serious injury. I've watched a comebacker hit a pitcher in the face, and it was scary. Here, the Woodchucks pitcher is quick—and lucky. He throws his gloved hand up almost instinctively in front of him, and the ball bounces off the glove and rolls slowly in the direction of first base. The pitcher has just enough time to run after the ball, field it with his throwing hand, and then flick it to first base to put the baserunner out before he arrives. One away.

The next two Grits batters go in quick succession; the center fielder pops up to the third baseman, and the right fielder strikes out. Three up and three down, or as you may hear someone calling the game say, "the side was retired in order."

Bottom of the Fifth

The Woodchucks go almost as quickly in the bottom of the fifth. The first batter up hits a long looping fly ball to the center fielder, who has to come in only a few steps to make the catch. This type of easily catchable fly ball is called "a can of corn." This archaic term comes from the late nineteenth or early twentieth century, when a grocer would use a stick with a hook on the end to retrieve a can from a shelf too high to reach by hand. The can would slide off the shelf and into the waiting arms of the grocer below; hence, the baseball is as easy to catch as a can of corn.

The second man up, the Woodchucks first baseman, hits a slow ground ball directly at the first baseman.

It should have been easy for the defender to make the play: He might run forward to field the bouncing ball and then dash over and touch the first base bag; or he might toss the ball to the pitcher, who has come off the mound and is dashing toward first base to catch the first baseman's toss and put the baserunner out. This should be a routine play, and the runner is almost always put out before he reaches first base. However, not this time. The first baseman fumbles (boots) the ball; it bounces through his legs and on out into right field. The Grits right fielder has come up closer to the infield; he retrieves the ball and throws it back to the first baseman, but the Woodchucks runner is safely on first. The official scorer charges the Grits first baseman with an error, and we see the error posted on the stadium scoreboard. Because this was scored as an error, the Woodchucks first baseman will not be credited with having made a hit.

The next Woodchucks batter, their left fielder, hits a fly ball to left field that looks like it is going to drop in front of the Grits left fielder before he can get to it. As soon as the ball is hit, the fielder is "on his horse," sprinting to where he thinks the baseball will land. It doesn't look like he will make it, but he keeps churning, until about ten feet from the ball he dives forward, arms extended and glove outstretched. Just before the ball hits the ground, the Grits left fielder gets his glove under it and . . . makes the catch as he continues to slide forward on his tummy over the still damp outfield. He rolls over and comes up covered with grass stains, and with his gloved hand thrust high into the air holding the baseball for all to see! One on and two away.

When the ball went sailing out into left field, the Woodchucks baserunner on first had gone back to the bag to tag up, and then waited to see if the Grits' left fielder would make the catch. When it looked to the baserunner like the left fielder didn't make the catch, the baserunner took off for second base. However, when he saw the outfielder come up with the ball, he skidded to a stop and sprinted back to first base to avoid making the third out to end the inning. Nonetheless, his caution is unrewarded, because the next batter, the Woodchucks center fielder, strikes out. Disappointment, like unpredictability, is an integral part of baseball. At the end of five, one Woodchucks baserunner is left stranded, and the score remains 5-3.

Sixth Inning

Top of the Sixth

The Woodchucks pitcher who came into the game in the third inning has caught fire and is pitching well. He "fans" or strikes out the first batter, the Grits left fielder, with four pitches. The next man up, the Grits pitcher, grounds out to second base on the first pitch. Then, the Grits shortstop swings at the first two pitches and misses, and takes the third pitch for a called strike. The top of the sixth is over in less than five minutes, so if you walked back under the stadium to the concession stands for a soda or a snack, you will have missed it. Better to wait if you can, since you'll have more time for a break in just a little while.

Bottom of the Sixth

The Woodchucks pitcher may have caught fire, but the Grits pitcher is about ready to be "lit up" (the meaning of the term in this context will become clear in just a moment) as the Woodchucks' bats come to life. The first batter, the Woodchucks catcher, hits a grounder into center field, up the alley between the Grits shortstop and second baseman into center field for a single. The next batter, the right fielder for the Woodchucks, earns a walk. The Woodchucks third baseman hits a double, driving in a run and putting the Woodchucks right fielder on third base. Sounds bad for the Grits pitcher, right? Well, things are about to go from bad to worse.

The next batter, the Woodchucks pitcher, gets into the act. He steps up to the plate and, out of nowhere, hits a home run. The fans around us are going crazy, as the Woodchucks have now scored four runs in the inning, with no outs, and lead the Grits 7 to 5. Since the batter was the Woodchucks pitcher and their weakest hitter, the Grits manager realizes that the bottom is falling out of the game for his pitcher. We see him turn to his pitching coach in the dugout and say something. We cannot hear him of course, but we can surmise that he is telling the pitching coach to "get someone up," meaning to call down on the bullpen phone and tell a relief pitcher to start warming up. The manager may have a particular reliever in mind, or he may tell the pitching coach to have a couple of pitchers warm up, depending on the circumstances.

Because we are only in the bottom of the sixth inning, it is too early to bring in the setup pitcher or the closer, so the manager will call on one of his middle-relievers. Most teams carry a half dozen or so relief pitchers, including the setup man and the closer, and there is usually at least one left-handed reliever on their pitching staff. The manager will make his pitching selection based on who the opposing team's upcoming batters will be. Generally, if the Woodchucks' batters are lefties, then the manager will select a right-handed pitcher; conversely, if the next batter (or batters) hit right-handed, the manager will summon a left-handed reliever.

The Woodchucks who are coming up to bat are a mix of left-handed batters and right-handed batters. The Grits manager could do a mix and match, bringing in a left-handed pitcher to pitch against one right-handed batter, and then a right-handed pitcher to go against a left-handed batter. However, he has great confidence in a particular right-handed reliever and he decides to go with him to get through the inning.

Unfortunately for the Grits, the pitcher won't have much time to get warmed up before he'll be called in from the bullpen. What happens next is a choreographed dance that is probably as old as baseball itself. The Grits manager motions from the dugout to the home plate umpire that he would like to go to the mound and speak with his pitcher, and the home plate umpire calls "time." While his relief pitcher tries to get loose out in the bullpen, the Grits manager slowly (oh so slowly) climbs the steps of the dugout and trudges out to the mound, accompanied by the pitching coach. The catcher and all the infield position players converge on the mound as well, and then the manager, the pitching coach, and the catcher chat with the pitcher and each other about . . . goodness knows what.

Generally, if a manager is thinking of leaving his pitcher in the game, he'll walk to the mound at a rapid pace. But every pitcher knows that when a manager slowly makes his way to the mound, the pitcher is likely "headed to the showers." Anyway, the conversation at the mound continues just so long as the home plate umpire will permit. At some point, he will walk out to the mound and tell the participants to break it up and play ball. The umpire knows that the decision has already been made to pull the pitcher, and that the manager is just stalling for time so that his reliever can adequately warm up before he enters the game.

At that point, the manager will reach out his hand, and the pitcher who is being relieved will hand the ball to him, and then the manager will officially summon his relief pitcher. After handing over the baseball, the pitcher being relieved will immediately leave the mound, and head to the dugout—none of the pitchers that leave a game are allowed to return to the game, so they do not go to the bullpen. One of the manager's main job responsibilities is to deal with player egos, and you will often see him give the exiting pitcher a pat on the shoulder or the fanny to let him know that everything is okay. If the manager has had both a right-handed and a left-handed pitcher warming up, he will signal which he wants in the game by touching that arm with his other hand; otherwise, he'll just beckon.

The reliever then comes out of the bullpen and heads for the pitcher's mound, where the Grits manager, coach and players gathered there await his arrival. When he gets there, the manager gives him the baseball, and a few instructions about how he wants the next batter to be pitched, and then the manager and everyone else head back to where they are supposed to be. The incoming pitcher makes his warm-up pitches, and the home plate umpire directs the players to play ball.

Turning back to our game, sometimes things just don't work out according to plan, and this is one of those times for the Grits manager. On the new pitcher's second pitch, the Woodchucks second baseman delivers the baseball into the outfield bleachers, giving the home team an 8 to 5 lead. The Woodchucks fans are gleeful, and they let their team know by roaring their approval. Some overzealous fans in the bleachers where the baseball landed start a "wave," standing up and throwing their arms above their heads and then sitting down, hoping that other fans nearby will follow suit so that the wave will ripple repeatedly around the stadium. However, most of the fans at the Burrow are focused on the game, and the wave peters out before it makes even one full circuit of the ballpark.

Irrespective of the home run that his pitcher just gave up, the Grits manager retains his confidence in his reliever, and hopes that he will settle down and get through the inning without allowing any further damage. The pitcher rises to the occasion, and in quick succession, the next three batters go down on a strike out, a ground out to the shortstop, and a fly out to left field. Since two of the three batters are the heart of the Woodchucks batting lineup, one might say that the reliever accomplished a minor miracle. So, at the end of six, the Woodchucks have 8 runs, 9 hits, and 0 errors, and the Grits have 5 runs, 8 hits, and 2 errors.

After the sixth inning, we see the grounds crew is back out on the ball field. They normally would tidy up the field after every three innings of play, but they didn't come out after the third inning today because they had just cleaned up after the rain delay in the middle of the inning. They haul the drags around the entire infield, and rake the ground around the bases, home plate, and the pitcher's mound. In some stadiums, the grounds crews actually do their work in a choreographed fashion, something like a line dance, to the accompaniment of taped music over the stadium's sound system, adding an element of entertainment to what would otherwise be a routine clean-up. Also, throughout the game, we have heard the strains of an organ being played over the Burrow's sound system. Organ music is a tradition in many stadiums, and some of the organists have become institutions in their own right.

The Late Innings

Seventh Inning

Top of the Seventh

The first batter up in the inning for the Grits is their the second baseman. He takes two balls and two called strikes, and then swings at a breaking ball down in the dirt for strike number three. One away.

Next up is the Grits catcher. He squares up and tries to bunt, but the ball skims just under the barrel of his bat. The manager then "takes off" the bunt by signaling to the third base coach, who passes the signal along to the batter that he can swing away at the next pitch. The pitcher, however, thinking that the bunt is probably still "on," throws a slider. The pitch heads off to the outside of the plate, away from the batter. The batter should have been more patient, but instead he "chases" the pitch, just getting the tip of his bat on the ball. As a result, he knocks a fast-moving and high-bouncing grounder down the third base line.

The baseball fates intervene to save the impatient batter from himself. The waiting third baseman misjudges where the hit ball will bounce, and "short-hops" it, meaning that he is too close to the ball when he fields it, and it comes up awkwardly into his glove—pressed against his chest. By the time he can get the ball into his throwing hand and ready to make the throw to first base, the Grits player is already "safely aboard" first base. Moments later, an "error" is flashed up on the scoreboard, meaning that the official scorer thinks that the Woodchuck's third baseman should have made the play. One on, and one away—and an error—and the Grits are still down 8-5.

The Grits first baseman steps up to the plate. He hits a foul ball out of play for a strike on the first pitch. On the second pitch, he hits a hard ground ball straight back at the pitcher. The Woodchucks pitcher jumps to get out of the way, but doesn't make it, and the ball hits him in the knee. He jerks and grimaces, seemingly in pain, but then scuttles quickly to the ball, which has come to rest against the grass at the edge of the dirt circle in front of the pitcher's mound. By this time, there is no play to be made at second base, so the pitcher throws it to first base for the only play possible. Two away.

Having successfully put the baserunner out, the pitcher flips off his glove, leans forward, and grabs his knee where the ball hit it. The Woodchucks manager, the pitching coach, and the team trainer rush out on the ball field to attend to the wounded player. After a few moments, the pitcher straightens up and walks around the mound. He reaches back, grabs his ankle with his hand, and pulls his leg up behind him a couple of times. He takes a few more steps and then nods his head up and down in the universal sign that he's okay—but his manager isn't buying it quite yet. Before he walks back to the dugout, the manager makes the pitcher throw a few pitches, while he and the pitching coach watch carefully as the pitcher goes through his throwing motion. Satisfied for the moment that their pitcher seems to be functioning without pain, the Woodchucks manager, coach, and trainer depart, while the next Grits batter, who has been taking practice swings just outside the batter's box, moves into the box and readies himself to hit.

The batter is the Grits third baseman. On a 2-1 count, he hits a foul ball that goes high into the air well outside of the right field foul line; it looks playable. The Woodchucks first baseman and right fielder both sprint toward where they think the ball will land, hoping to catch it and put the batter out. However, a breeze catches the baseball and pulls it rightward; unplayable, the ball lands several rows back in the stands. The count is now 2-2.

On the next pitch, the batter hits another foul ball, but this time the ball pops high in the air behind the catcher, beyond home plate but in front of the backstop—a playable foul ball. The home plate umpire steps out of the way as the Woodchucks catcher jumps up from his crouch and flings his mask aside. The catcher backpedals, keeping his eye on the ball as he moves, his arms raised to shoulder height with his mitt turned skyward. He sidesteps to the right, oblivious to everything except the baseball. After what seems like an eternity, the ball descends into his waiting mitt. Three away! As the crowd applauds, the catcher quietly hands the baseball to the umpire, retrieves his mask, and heads to the dugout.

The Seventh Inning Stretch

It is now time for the Seventh Inning Stretch. Like many things about baseball, no one is quite certain of its origin. What is known is that the Seventh Inning Stretch has been around for well over a century, and it is one of professional baseball's better-known traditions. When I was growing up, the Seventh Inning Stretch was solely a joyful event—especially if our team was in the lead! We had an opportunity to stand up and stretch, to head to one of the concession stands for goodies, or to visit the public facilities. If we stayed at our seats, we could stand and join with the other spectators in singing what I can only describe as the national anthem of baseball, "Take Me Out to the Ballgame." The lyrics are flashed up on one of the large electronic boards in the stadium, and the chorus goes like this:

Take me out to the ball game,
Take me out with the crowd;
Buy me some peanuts and Cracker Jack,
I don't care if I never get back.
Let me root, root, root for the home team,
If they don't win, it's a shame.
For its one, two, three strikes, you're out,
At the old ball game.

After the tragedy on September 11, 2001, another song found its way into the Seventh Inning Stretch. Once the crowd sings "Take Me Out to the Ballgame," "God Bless America" is now sung in some stadiums at every game, often performed by a famous singer, and the crowd stands for the occasion. At our game today, we look out on the ball field and see the four umpires lined up beyond the pitcher's mound, facing the American flag beyond the outfield wall, caps off and held over their hearts, as a local singer leads us in the song. We join together in saluting those who perished on that awful day.

Bottom of the Seventh

The Woodchucks come up to bat in the bottom of the seventh inning with a three-run lead. As you recall, after giving up a home run, the Grits relief pitcher righted himself, and put out two of the three batters in the heart of the Woodchucks' lineup to get out of the inning. Now, however, he doesn't fare quite so well. The first two batters hit him for singles, putting the Woodchucks center fielder and catcher on first and second base. The Grits pitcher then unintentionally walks the Woodchucks right fielder to load the bases. No outs and the bases are loaded; things don't look too good for the Grits pitcher. However, he is about to get some unexpected help from his second baseman.

The Woodchucks third baseman comes to the plate. He lets the first three pitches go by, and earns a 1-2 count. On the fourth pitch, the pitcher "jams" the batter, meaning the pitch is high and inside, and difficult to hit. However, the Woodchucks batter has two strikes, and the pitch looks to him to be in the strike zone. He doesn't want to go down on a called strike, so he comes around with his bat to "fight off the pitch," hoping to knock it foul and avoid being put out. He connects with the ball low on the bat barrel, down where it starts to taper. As a result, the batter gets just enough wood on the ball to hit it directly to the Grits second baseman, who makes the easy catch, and then tags the Woodchucks baserunner coming from first base, putting him out. The first two put-outs happen so quickly that the Woodchucks baserunner on second, who had been leading off the bag toward third base, doesn't have time to react, and the Grits second baseman touches second base before the baserunner can dive back to the bag. We have just seen the Grits second baseman "turn" an unassisted triple play—where one defensive player puts three offensive players out—one of the rarest plays in baseball.

How rare is an unassisted triple play? Let me put this in perspective. What I will call an "assisted" triple play involves two or more defensive players throwing the ball to each other to put baserunners out. Each year, fewer than a half dozen triple plays of this type are made throughout the major league baseball season. By comparison, there have been only fifteen unassisted triple plays in major league baseball since 1909. It is fair to say that the unassisted triple play is baseball's equivalent to Stravinsky's mythical and elusive Firebird—rarely seen and difficult to capture.

An unassisted triple play will happen very fast. I have never seen an unassisted triple play, but I happened to hear one once on the radio as it was happening. It was Memorial Day, 2000. The New York Yankees and the Oakland Athletics were playing the first of a three-game series at Yankee Stadium. The game was going along relatively quietly, and at the bottom of the sixth inning there were Yankee baserunners on first and second. Out of nowhere, the A's second baseman caught a soft line drive, tagged out the Yankee baserunner coming from first, and then tagged second base before the Yankee baserunner who had been on second could get back to the bag—an unassisted triple play: it happened in about the time it just took you to read it. At the time, I didn't realize what a rarity an unassisted triple play was; it was only later that I understood the significance of what I had heard that day.

Eighth Inning

Top of the Eighth

The Grits are running out of innings. They are down to six outs and they need to score 3 runs to tie, and at least 4 runs to win the game. The sixth batter in the Grits lineup, their centerfielder, is coming up to bat to lead off in the inning. If the Grits batters "go in order" during the eighth and ninth innings (each is put out in turn as they come up to bat over the next two innings) the Grits would not get back around to their power hitters before the game would be over. The Grits pitcher is scheduled to be the fourth batter in the inning, and the manager has already decided that he will put in a pinch hitter to replace him when it is his turn to bat.

Meanwhile, up at bat, the Grits center fielder takes a ball just off the outside corner of the plate for a 1-0 count. He swings at the next pitch, smacking a long high fly ball to the deepest part of centerfield. The Woodchucks center fielder races back to the outfield wall, glove outstretched to make the catch—but he can't get to the ball before it hits the wall and bounces away from him. By the time the Woodchucks left fielder can get to the baseball and throw it back in to his second baseman, the Grits center fielder has already arrived there safely.

The Grits right fielder steps into the batter's box. The Woodchucks pitcher starts him off with his trademark pitch—a cutter that breaks high and inside, up "in the batter's kitchen." The only thing that the Grits batter can do with the pitch is to fight it off. He does, but his bat shatters when he makes contact with the ball low on the bat barrel. The force of the hit is just enough to propel the ball in a soft little pop fly back to the pitcher, who makes the catch for the first out. One away.

The third batter in the inning is the Grits left fielder. The batter takes the first two pitches, both cutters, for strikes. For his third pitch, the pitcher decides to show the batter something different, and throws him a change-up—an off-speed pitch. The pitcher meant to throw it down low, which would have made it more difficult to hit, but instead the ball stays high (hangs) as it closes on home plate. The batter takes a good cut at the baseball, connects, and sends it sailing down along the left field line, where it bounces from fair territory into foul territory well past third base, takes a hop, and then heads into the corner where the wall in front of the left field stands meets the outfield wall. The left fielder goes after it, thinking to field it as it caroms off the two walls, playing the angles like a billiard player. However, the ball fools him; it bounces up under a slight overhang at the base of the outfield wall and comes to a dead stop. As he hurries to collect the ball and return it to the infield, the Grits batter-baserunner rounds first and heads for second. Meanwhile, the Grits baserunner on second base has sprinted to third base; the third base coach is watching what is going on in the outfield, and holds the baserunner there. As the Woodchucks left fielder gets his hands on the baseball and throws it back to his third baseman, the Grits batter-baserunner goes into second base standing up. With only one away, there are now Grits runners on second and third.

With a Grits pinch hitter coming to bat in place of the pitcher that was taken out, the Woodchucks manager appears to be getting worried. He calls for time and goes out to talk with his pitcher, planning to give him some encouragement and some guidance on how to pitch to the next batter. He walks up onto the mound, and the Woodchucks position players in the infield gather around to hear what's being said. After a few words, the manager turns and makes his way off the mound, heading back toward his dugout. He's gone perhaps five feet from the edge of the dirt circle at the base of the pitcher's mound and onto the infield grass when one of the position players still standing on the mound calls after him. Before stopping to think, the manager turns and walks back into the dirt circle and halfway up on to the mound. Bad idea.

The manager of the Grits jumps out of his dugout, yelling to the home plate umpire like he's just seen a crime committed. The umpire already knows what he is yelling about; in fact, the umpire had been shouting at the Woodchucks manager not to go back into the dirt circle at the base of the mound, but the manager didn't hear him. Under MLB rules, if a manager makes two trips to the mound in one inning to the same pitcher, he is required to remove that pitcher—and when the manager steps from the infield grass back onto the dirt around the mound, that counts as a second trip. This turn of events puts the Woodchucks in a bind. No Woodchucks pitchers had been warming up in the bullpen, so no one is ready to come into the ballgame in relief. While the Woodchucks manager argues with the umpire, the pitching coach hurriedly calls down to the bullpen to get someone loosened up. The pitching coach decides to go with his setup man.

Normally, the Woodchucks setup pitcher would be sitting this game out; the relief pitcher already in the game was doing fine, and the Woodchucks seemed to be cruising along with a comfortable 3-run lead. However, the Woodchucks starters have been pitching into the late innings over the past few games, and the setup pitcher can use the work. Nonetheless, he would have preferred not to come into the game under these circumstances.

After only a couple of throws in the bullpen, the setup pitcher is hurried into the game. Once he gets to the mound, he is allowed the eight warm-up pitches mandated by MLB rules—not nearly enough—before the home plate umpire orders the men to play ball.

The Grits pinch hitter steps into the batter's box knowing that the Woodchucks pitcher is still not adequately warmed up and ready to face him. He takes the first couple of pitches without swinging, waiting to see if the pitcher can get the ball over the plate. A seasoned veteran, this ain't the Woodchucks pitcher's first rodeo, and he knows what the batter is up to. Even so, the pitcher is having control problems, and he throws the batter three consecutive balls. Behind in the count 3-0, and wanting to get out of the inning without putting any more Grits on base, the pitcher makes a mistake. He sends a pitch right down the pipe, and the batter "jacks" the baseball high into the air and out over the left field wall. A collective groan arises from the crowd as the Grits baserunners round the bases and head for home. With one swing, the pinch hitter has tied the game.

The pitcher is obviously shaken, but he has little time to recover, because the next batter, the Grits shortstop, has already come to the plate.[8] The pitcher throws a high outside pitch off the corner of the plate, and the batter chases it, popping it into the waiting glove of the Woodchucks first baseman. The Grits second baseman steps into the batter's box next. He hits a hard grounder into the hole up the middle of the infield, just to the left of second base. Unfortunately for the batter, the Woodchucks second baseman is playing close to the bag. The fielder dives for the ball and makes an unbelievable stop; springing to his feet, he zips the ball to the Woodchucks first baseman for the third out. The Grits side is retired, but the damage has been done—the score is now 8-8.

Bottom of the Eighth

Because the Grits have tied the game, their manager decides to gamble; he brings in his closer to shut down the Woodchucks, hoping that his team can pull ahead in the top of the ninth inning, and then hold on to win the game.

---

[8] There is a certain relentless quality to baseball, when you consider that the batters just keep coming up to bat until they make three outs and their side is retired. Along those lines, there is no "mercy" rule in MLB that allows an official to call a game when the score becomes too lopsided. Since 1900, the most lopsided MLB game played was in 2007, when the Texas Rangers whipped the Baltimore Orioles 30-3. Why isn't there a mercy rule? Because MLB games don't have time limits, it is possible that a team can come back from being way behind (meaning ten runs or more) in the late innings and win. It happens.

The first Woodchucks batter is a pinch hitter, coming into the game in place of the Woodchucks pitcher. At this point in the game and under these circumstances, this is not an unexpected move. The pinch hitter knocks a ground ball through the gap between the third baseman and the shortstop for a single. The next batter, the Woodchucks second baseman, hits a flare that is just over the outstretched glove of the Grits shortstop for another single. Now we have Woodchucks baserunners on first and second, with no one out.

Then, the Grits closer bears down. He strikes out the Woodchucks shortstop, and then gets the Woodchucks first baseman to ground out to first. Two out, and two men on base.

Next up is the fourth man in the Woodchucks batting order, the left fielder. The batter takes the pitcher to a full count (3-2). When the count was at 2-2, the baserunners on first and second both took off and ran to second and third base. The pitcher and catcher, concentrating on getting the batter out, clearly ignored them. Consequently the official scorer did not credit them with stealing bases, but instead scored their movement as "defensive indifference." In any event, the batter flies out to right field on the next pitch, so the baserunners' efforts to advance were for naught.

The Grits manager gambled, and the gamble has paid off—so far. His closer did his job, and got through the bottom of the eighth inning without giving up a run. Now, it's up to the Grits batters to score some runs to pull ahead; if they can, the closer only has to get through the bottom of the ninth inning unscathed for the Grits to win.

The Ninth Inning

Top of the Ninth

The Grits' bats came alive in the eighth inning. The Woodchucks manager wants to hold them in check, hoping that his players can score in the bottom of the ninth and end the game. He brings in his closer to shut the Grits batters down.

Back at the beginning of this book, I told you that unlike other American professional team sports, there is no "sudden death" in baseball. That is true. However, if an MLB team playing at home is ahead at the conclusion of the top half of the ninth inning, the game is over. This may seem obvious, because if the visiting team is behind at that point, they don't get another chance to bat. However, probably because it doesn't have the comforting symmetry of a complete inning being played, it may be a little jarring the first time you see it happen.

In any event, the first Grits batter to come up in the top of the ninth inning is their catcher; he is the third batter in the Grits lineup, and the beginning of the heart of their batting order. Nonetheless, the Woodchucks closer promptly and efficiently puts him away with three strikes on four pitches. The Woodchucks fans are happy-happy, and they let their closer know it.

In baseball as in life, sometimes things don't quite work out according to plan. It made perfect sense to bring in the closer, but even the best of closers occasionally gets "rocked" (meaning that the other team feasts on his pitches), just like every other pitcher in baseball. The next batter up is the Grits "primo" power hitter, the first baseman. He lets the first two pitches go by, and then slams a towering home run high up into the left field stands for the go-ahead run. Grits 9, Woodchucks 8.

The Grits third baseman, another power hitter, comes up to bat next. For obvious reasons, the Woodchucks closer is wary of him. The batter takes the first pitch high and outside, and the second pitch low and outside, for a 2-0 count. Now, the batter is ahead of the pitcher, and he knows that the pitcher will likely throw him something that he can hit. The pitcher throws him a breaking ball over the plate, but he isn't able to keep it down far enough—and the batter makes him pay. He hits a flare over the second baseman for a single. The Woodchucks closer strolls off the back of the mound; he reaches down and picks up the rosin bag laying there, clearly stalling for time to give himself an opportunity to steady his nerves.

The Grits center fielder comes up for the fifth time in the game. The Woodchucks closer throws him a fastball, and he hits a stinging line drive down the third base line. The Woodchucks third baseman was standing seven to eight feet off the bag, and he flings himself at the ball, knocking it to the ground with his glove. Bouncing up, he grabs the ball and fires it to the second baseman. In what is called a "bang-bang" play, the baserunner slides into second base just a half-second ahead of the defender's catch, and looks up at the second base umpire, expectantly awaiting the call he wants to hear. "Safe!" shouts the umpire, as he signals the call by spreading his arms wide. Still only one out, with Grits runners now on first and second.

The Woodchucks fans are getting restless because their closer is looking shaky. The Woodchucks catcher is also concerned, and he asks for time and heads out to the mound to calm his pitcher. We'll know in a moment if the catcher accomplished his goal. The next batter up is the Grits right fielder. He doesn't swing at the first pitch, but he drives the baseball high and far on the second pitch, almost to the right centerfield wall. The Woodchucks' center fielder and right fielder both take off in a flat-out sprint for the ball, eyes skyward, concentrating on making the catch, unaware that they are heading directly for each other. They suddenly realize what is about to happen just before they collide—too late to avoid the collision, but not too late to twist their bodies and lessen the impact. Both fielders go down, and the baseball hits the ground. The centerfielder is dazed, but the right fielder collects himself quickly. He springs up, scrambles for the ball, and hurls it to the waiting second baseman.

The Grits baserunners on first and second base took off running when they saw the baseball hit the ground. The Grits baserunner who had been on second crosses the plate standing up, while the baserunner behind him has rounded third base, following hard on his heels. The Woodchucks second baseman turns toward home plate, sees that he has a chance to make the play, and fires the ball to his catcher.

Just as the Grits catcher did back in the second inning, the Woodchucks catcher covers home plate with his body and prepares to make the catch and put the baserunner out. Good idea, if the throw from second is accurate—it isn't. The throw comes in to home plate behind (to the right) of the catcher. To make the catch, the catcher is pulled off home plate, and the runner slides in safely. The Grits now lead the Woodchucks 11-8, and still have only one out.

All the closer wants to do now is stop the bleeding— to get out of the inning without giving up another run. Meanwhile another potential run for the Grits is standing out at second base; the player who just got the hit has sneaked over from first while all the action was going on at home plate.

The next batter is the Grits left fielder. With only one out in the inning, the Grits manager signals for the batter to swing away. He does—but to no avail. He hits a ground ball to the shortstop, who fields it and makes an almost too-short throw to first base, which the first baseman reaches for and digs out of the ground for the second Grits out in the inning. The Grits closer comes to the plate next. He rarely gets up to bat, and he proves to be the easy out one would expect him to be, taking three strikes on five pitches to end the Grits at-bats. All in all, the top of the ninth was a very good half-inning for the Grits. However, the fans at the Burrow, who had been upbeat and boisterous all afternoon while their team was leading, have now grown quiet.

Bottom of the Ninth

The Woodchucks are stunned. They are not used to their closer giving up runs. They had been ahead or tied for much of the game, and now in the bottom of the ninth, down to three outs, they suddenly find themselves down by three runs. To make matters worse, after their first two batters (the Woodchucks center fielder and catcher), the weaker hitters in their lineup (the right fielder and the third baseman) are scheduled to bat. From a Woodchucks perspective, things aren't looking too good right now.

The Woodchucks center fielder hits a little flare, just over the head of the second baseman, for a single. The Woodchucks have new life—their leadoff batter in the inning is on base, and they have no outs. The noise around us starts to build as the Woodchucks fans expectantly urge their team on.

The next batter, the Woodchucks catcher, hits a ground ball toward the gap between first and second base, and the Grits second baseman scurries to field the ball. The Woodchucks baserunner on first base had taken a substantial lead, and as he makes tracks toward second base the baseball bounces up and hits him in the shin of his trailing leg, deflecting the ball in a direction that makes it unplayable.

The second base umpire has been intently watching the Woodchucks baserunner coming toward him, and he reacts immediately after he sees the ball hit the runner—pointing with his left hand at the baserunner, and screaming "You're out!" as he pumps his right fist. Why is the baserunner out? The Woodchucks baserunner is not allowed to interfere with the hit baseball, and if he does, he is automatically out. Also, if the umpire had determined that the baserunner interfered with the ball with the obvious intention of breaking up a double play, the umpire could have ruled the batter/baserunner out as well. Fortunately for the Woodchucks, the umpire didn't think the Grits second baseman would have been able to turn a double play. Now we have one away in the bottom of the ninth, and a Woodchucks baserunner on first. Meanwhile, the Woodchucks fans around us are united in loudly expressing their view of the umpire's call in quite unflattering terms.

The Woodchucks right fielder bats next. Although the batter is not, overall, a particularly strong hitter, he has a record of success against the Grits closer, and the closer remembers that this batter has hit him hard.

The Grits manager knows this as well. The pitcher, as would almost any self-respecting pitcher, wants to try and put the batter out. However, the manager doesn't want to take a chance on that happening, and he instructs the pitcher to "work around" the batter so that he can get to the weaker bats to follow.

The Grits manager also knows that the Woodchucks right fielder does not have a lot of foot speed, and with the eighth batter in the Woodchucks batting order coming to the plate next, the manager would rather have the right fielder on first base than the Woodchucks catcher, who is currently there. The Woodchucks catcher is a better baserunner than the right fielder; he is also a more physical baserunner, and could more likely break up the double play that the Grits manager is angling to set up so as to get out of the inning with a win. The manager signals what he wants done through the catcher to his pitcher, who, not surprisingly, is not too happy about this instruction. Still, the pitcher does what he is told and walks the Woodchucks right fielder. One out in the bottom of the ninth inning with the Grits holding onto a three-run lead, and now we have Woodchucks baserunners on first and second.

The Woodchucks third baseman steps into the batter's box. Aside from the Woodchucks pitcher, who is due to bat next, this hitter is the weakest bat in the Woodchucks' lineup. The Grits closer bears down, and after setting the batter up with two high fastballs, gets him to swing—weakly—at an off-speed pitch that the batter pops into the glove of the Grits third baseman. Two away, and the Woodchucks fans are really getting restless.

The next batter up is supposed to be the Woodchucks closer, but it's time for the Woodchucks manager to change things up. It is in situations like this where the manager truly earns his salary. Let's think this through with him: Should he substitute another player for the closer? His team is down by three runs, and he has only one out remaining to get back into the game. His weakest batter is about to come up to the plate, and he will likely be an easy out to end the game. Assuming nevertheless that his team can come back to tie the score, the Woodchucks manager would love to have his closer remain in the game to stop the other team from scoring during the extra innings. However, he realizes that by retaining the closer in his lineup, the chances of the Woodchucks getting into extra innings are slim and none—and slim has already left town.

The Woodchucks manager decides to substitued one of his "bench players" who has been sitting in the dugout for his closer/next batter. The Woodchucks manager looks over his roster, and picks one of his backup utility fielders—a former starter on the downside of his career, yet still a formidable batter—to pinch hit for the closer.

Meanwhile, the Grits manager is not placidly sitting over there in his dugout on the other side of the ball field contemplating the existential meaning of life, ignoring what the Woodchucks manager is up to. When he sees that the Woodchucks are pulling their closer from the batting lineup and bringing in a pinch hitter, he immediately counters by instructing his pitcher to walk the new batter intentionally.

Intentional walks are choreographed affairs. The Woodchucks batter knows (or quickly figures out) what is coming, and he stands in the batter's box, bat at the ready, just in case the Grits pitcher should change his mind. The catcher is required by rule to be within the catcher's box when the pitcher is pitching; otherwise a balk will be called on the pitcher. So, the catcher stands in his box and stretches his arm out to his side, away from the batter, as a target for the pitcher. The pitcher then throws the ball—it's actually more like a toss—to the catcher, who steps out of the catcher's box for each throw to get squarely in front of the oncoming ball. The walked batter tosses his bat to the side and trots to first base. We still have two outs in the bottom of the ninth inning, and now the bases are loaded with Woodchucks.

The next two Woodchucks scheduled to bat in the inning are the first two batters at the top of their lineup; respectively, the second baseman and the shortstop. Neither one of these batters should be as difficult to put out as the batter who was just intentionally walked.

The Woodchucks second baseman's at-bat doesn't quite go the way that the Grits thought it would. The Grits fielders knew the batter was unlikely to hit a long ball, so they had already moved in closer to the infield to better their chances of making a play on the ball. Also, because the batter is right-handed, as most second basemen are, the Grits catcher had repositioned the fielders, shifting the Grits players slightly to the left, again with the thought that this would better their chances of making a play.

The batter has seen that the shift was put on. Normally this hitter chokes up on his bat a bit, hoping that he can drive a hit baseball into shallow left field, or through the gaps in the left side of the infield. However, when he sees that the shift has been put on and the Grits defensive players have been moved over to cover where they think he will hit, he grasps the bat down close to the knob, thinking that if he can get wood on the ball farther up the barrel, he can drive the ball toward right field, ideally down along the first base line and away from the defending Grits. The pitcher's second pitch is a curveball that the batter probably should have passed up. Instead, he takes a cut at it, and drives it into shallow right field, where it lands in front of and to the left of the right fielder. Before the Grits right fielder can recover the baseball, the Woodchucks baserunner on third heads for home, cutting the Grits' lead to two. By the time the Grits right fielder comes up with the ball, he sees he has no play on any of the bases, and he throws the ball into his catcher—to make sure no other runs score. The bases are again loaded with Woodchucks runners, and the Grits are just hoping to hang on.

A few moments earlier, when the Woodchucks were still down by three runs, and down to their final out, you could hear a buzzing in the Burrow from their nervous fans. Now, they are roaring their support as the Woodchucks shortstop walks to the plate. He takes the first pitch, a cutter, for a strike. The din in the stadium grows louder. The batter takes the second pitch, a breaking ball down in the dirt, for a ball. The batter is sitting on a count of 1-1. He does not swing at the next two pitches, both balls, so now the count is 3-1.

You can almost feel the tension in the stadium. The coaches and the players on both teams are up off the benches in their respective dugouts, draped over the protective barrier that separates the dugout from the field. The Woodchucks fans are on their feet as well, screaming encouragement to the batter.

The batter swings at the next pitch, a curveball, with all of his might, fouling it down and away as he comes around so hard that you'd think he was trying to screw himself into the ground. Strike two! Although it doesn't seem possible, the crowd noise gets louder. A full count; now neither the pitcher nor the batter has any margin for error.

As the Woodchucks batter collects himself, the Grits pitcher makes a fateful decision. He decides to see if he can throw a fastball past the batter and end this game now. As he winds up, the fans are going crazy. The pitcher rears back and throws, sending a 96 mile-per-hour fastball straight down the pipe. The batter swings—and you can hear the crack of his bat connecting with the ball even over the din of the crowd. The ball lifts in a glorious arc high over center field.

The Grits center fielder, now back near the wall, stands and looks up helplessly as the ball passes high over him, leaves the ball field, and finally comes down about twenty rows up in the stands, in the midst of a waiting crowd of eager fans who are all reaching for the ball simultaneously.

Ladies and gentlemen you have just witnessed a walk-off "grand slam" (meaning the bases were loaded with baserunners when the batter hit the homer) home run to end the ballgame: it's all over and done; end of story; the Woodchucks win. The Woodchucks baserunners round the bases, being careful to touch every base as they pass, as required by MLB rules. They each cross home plate, and turn to wait for their shortstop who is coming into home behind them— wearing a grin so big that even we can see it! The Woodchucks in the dugout run out to join their fellow players at home plate. Just before the Woodchucks shortstop gets to home plate, he flings off his batting helmet and then leaps forward into the arms of his waiting teammates.

So what is the final score? The three Woodchucks players who were already on base cross home plate to score in front of the man who hit the walk-off home run, so that means the Woodchucks scored five runs in the bottom of the ninth, to win with 13 runs, 16 hits, and one error, while the Grits lose with 11 runs, 16 hits, and two errors. The scoreboard looks like this:

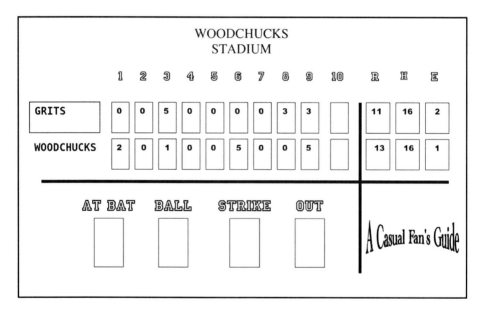

		1	2	3	4	5	6	7	8	9	10	R	H	E
GRITS		0	0	5	0	0	0	0	3	3		11	16	2
WOODCHUCKS		2	0	1	0	0	5	0	0	5		13	16	1

WOODCHUCKS STADIUM

AT BAT   BALL   STRIKE   OUT

A Casual Fan's Guide

We watch as the Woodchucks manager and coaches line up in single file out on the ball field. In front of them, the Woodchucks players (everyone who played in the game, the bench players, and the pitchers from the bullpen), line up in single file. The two lines walk forward, meet and pass each other, each person giving the man passing him a "high-five." The game is over, and as the participants leave the field, we join the joyous throngs of Woodchucks fans as they flow out of the Burrow.

Thanks for coming with me, and I hope you had as good a time as I did. Maybe we'll see each other at another game up the road. Take care.

Chapter 9

Covering More Bases

Here are some aspects of baseball that I didn't otherwise discuss or present in the game we went to.

- **"Extra Innings"**—I referenced extra innings a couple of times earlier in the book, and they are always a possibility. In fact, I just went to a game that was tied at the end of nine innings, lasted twelve innings, and ended in the bottom of the twelfth with a walk-off home run. Remember that the home team will always get its at-bats in the bottom of an extra inning, but the extra inning will end at any point when the home team scores a run that puts it ahead, even if there are not yet any outs in that half of the inning.

- **A "Perfect Game"**—A perfect game is a game in which a pitcher does not allow any batter from the other team to get on base during the entire game. Saying a pitcher has pitched a perfect game doesn't mean that he struck out twenty-seven batters in a row; in a perfect game, a batter can ground out, fly out, or be struck out. In a perfect game, not one player from the other team even got to first base by any means: by getting a hit, earning a walk, or being hit by a ball.

As of October 2012, only 23 perfect games had been pitched since 1880. Although perfect games have been less rare in the past few seasons, they still come along only once in a blue moon. I always like to put things in a timeline perspective, so let's try this: There are thirty MLB teams, and during the regular season each team plays five or six games a week. If you multiply five (games) times fifteen (when the thirty teams are paired off to play), about seventy-five games are played each week during the season—or over three times the total number of perfect games that have been pitched in 132 years. My point is that even with more perfect games being pitched these days, they ain't everyday happenings. I hope you get to see one someday.

- **A "No-Hitter"**—A no-hitter (or a no-hit ball game) is a game where the pitcher (or less frequently, multiple pitchers) does not give up a hit during the game. He can walk a batter, or put the batter on base by hitting him with the baseball, but the pitcher does not give up a hit. No-hitters are rare, but not nearly as rare as a perfect game; no-hitters happen roughly a couple of times a season. Also, a pitcher can throw a no-hitter and still lose a ballgame—it's happened—by walking batters or hitting them with a baseball and putting them on base, and/or through fielding errors.

No-hitters and perfect games can start out the same (actually, a perfect game is also included under the umbrella of a no-hitter), because a pitcher may not allow any opposing batter to get on base for several innings. As the innings progress and no players get on base, two things will happen: (1) "electricity" will start to build in the stadium, and it will go quiet as the knowledgeable fans begin to realize what they are seeing; and (2) you will get to see one of the more interesting superstitions in baseball, as no one talks to the pitcher throwing the no-hitter; everyone shies away from him in the dugout when his team is on offense. Also, you are not supposed to mention that you are seeing a no-hitter (same goes for a perfect game) while it is in process. However, once the pitcher finishes throwing a no-hitter, his teammates mob him, and the fans in the stands erupt in noise.

- **A "Shutout"**—A shutout is where the pitcher (or pitchers, if the starting pitcher is relieved) does not give up a run. A perfect game would also be a shutout.

- **"Hitting for the Cycle"**—If a batter hits a single, a double, a triple, and a home run, all in one game, he has hit for the cycle. The hits do not have to be in the order set out above, so he could hit the double in his first at-bat, and the single in his fourth at-bat. Still, it is a rare feat for a player to hit for the cycle.

- **A "Triple"**—Hitting a triple puts the batter/base runner at third base. A triple is, in my opinion, the second most difficult hit to make. The hitter/baserunner has to get all the way to third base having hit a baseball that doesn't leave the ball field—and is therefore (unlike a home run) in play the entire time he is running the bases. For a player to hit a triple, generally there is another baserunner (or multiple baserunners) already on base, most often on second base (in scoring position) or third base, and the defense is concentrating on stopping that baserunner from scoring. Also, the batter hitting the triple has to be fleet of foot, and most likely he has hit the baseball somewhere into the outfield where it is difficult for the outfielder to quickly recover and return it to the infield.

- **An "Inside-the-Park Home Run"**—The most difficult hit to make. The baseball never leaves the ball field, and is therefore in play while the baserunner rounds the bases and scores.

- **"Hit and Run"**—Most often, there is a baserunner on first base (although the baserunner could be on second or third base), and he runs for second when the batter hits the ball—hopefully to somewhere that pulls the second baseman away from the base so that the baserunner can get there safely. Rather a risky play, because the batter has to get some sort of a hit, but if it works it keeps the defense from turning a double play.

- **A "Foul Tip"**—A foul tip is where the batter gets a piece of the ball with the bat as the ball goes past him, straight back into the catcher's mitt—and is caught. Hypothetically, let's say that the batter gets three foul tips in a row. All three foul tips would be strikes, so the batter will be out after the third foul tip. One would think that a foul tip would be treated like any other foul ball; regardless of the count, if it's caught in the air before it hits the ground, the batter should be out. The best logical explanation I can come up with for why the first two foul tips are strikes is because it would discourage a batter from swinging at a pitch if he thought that getting any of the bat on it could be an immediate out, thereby giving an unfair advantage to the pitcher.

- **An Odd Home Run**—During our game, I told you about the ground-rule double, where a hit baseball that bounces through the outfield and over the outfield wall will be ruled a double. However, if a hit baseball bounces off the head of an outfielder and over the fence, it's a home run! Why? Because the baseball never touched the ground. This actually happened in a game between the Texas Rangers and the Cleveland Indians in 1993.

- **A Do-Over**—Let's say a batter is up at the plate with two outs and a baserunner on first base. The batter has a count of 2-2, and the baserunner on first decides to steal second base—and is put out to make the third out that ends the inning. What happens to the batter who is standing there with the 2-2 count? He then becomes the first batter up when his team next comes up to bat, with his balls and strikes erased. That's right; he starts all over again with a count of 0-0.

- **Keeping Score With a Scorecard**—Keeping score is something that you might like to try when you go to the ballpark to see a game. The essence of keeping score with a scorecard is that each position player is designated by a number, so when a player, or a combination of players, makes a play, you mark down the numerical designations on the scorecard—a copy of which will be in a program that you can purchase at the ballpark. The program will give you simple instructions about how to keep score, and if you fill in the information on the scorecard you will have a complete record of what happened throughout the game. Many years ago, I was shown how to keep score, but I find it gets in the way of my watching what is going on out on the field. An alternative perspective is that scoring the game helps you stay more involved.

- **Statistics**—If you are a numbers person, then baseball is the game for you! If you listen to a game on the radio or watch on television, in addition to important statistical information, you will hear some of the most obscure statistics cited that you have ever heard with respect to any field of human endeavor. Something like "This batter is the first batter to go 0-4 in games played on consecutive Tuesdays in the month of August in San Diego during interleague play" is admittedly a bit of hyperbole—but not by much. Watch and listen, and I guarantee you'll hear a statistic that makes you stop and say "Huh?" Not to worry; some folks really enjoy looking up and/or quoting obscure factoids and statistics, and if that's your thing, then there is plenty here for you to enjoy. Having said that, baseball really is "a game of averages," because one looks to see how a team or a player performs over time to understand what their future performance will likely be. Earlier in the book, I covered some of the significant statistical data points used for analyses, such as earned run averages, batting averages, and on-base percentages, so you'll have the basics down when you go to a ballgame.

- **Multiple Back-to-Back Home Runs**—I once watched on television as the Los Angeles Dodgers came from behind in the bottom of the ninth inning to hit four home runs in a row and tie the San Diego Padres—and then hit a walk-off home run in the tenth inning to win the game (and yes, the Padres did change pitchers to try to stop all this from happening). Speaking of statistics, four home runs in a row is an event that has happened seven times in MLB history, and we are still waiting for a team to hit five home runs in a row. Heck, we just might see this happen, but I'm not planning on holding my breath until it does!

Chapter 10

Some MLB History, Organization and Structure, and the Playoffs

Let's start at the beginning, with the origin of baseball. Once upon a time . . . actually, you get to decide which story you like best! Some folks claim that baseball came from England or elsewhere in Europe; some claim that the game was originated by Native Americans; and others claim that it was originated by Civil War general Abner Doubleday in Cooperstown, New York. In fact, MLB put together a commission in the early 1900s, and it decided that Doubleday was the inventor. The Doubleday story is actually my favorite, because it touches on other pieces of our history. Doubleday is larger than life: He ordered the first Union artillery shot that was fired from Fort Sumter in 1861 (literally at the very beginning of the Civil War); he fought at the battle of Gettysburg; and he is credited with having written "Taps," the most haunting and beautiful melody that I have ever heard. The extended Doubleday family also has an interesting link with baseball history; in the 1890s, a Doubleday was a founder of a publishing company that would go on to purchase the New York Mets (originally named the "New York Metropolitans") baseball team in 1980.

In any event, the commission (the "Spaulding Commission"—you will recognize the name Spaulding if you play almost any sport in the United States) decided that Doubleday invented the modern game of baseball in the little village of Cooperstown, New York, in 1839. Hence, the National Baseball Hall of Fame and Museum (the "Hall of Fame") was established in Cooperstown in 1936. Subsequently, MLB players who meet the qualifications (only the best of the best) have been elected to the Hall of Fame. The members of the Baseball Writers' Association of America (the "BBWAA") vote on who gets in, and they even have a committee for consideration of players who played in the days before the Hall of Fame came into being.

The game of baseball didn't gain prominence in the United States until after the Civil War, when the first professional team, the Cincinnati Red Stockings, took the field in the late 1860s. In 1871, the National Association of Professional Base Ball Players was founded, and in 1876, the National League replaced it. In 1901, the American League was founded, and these two leagues survive to this day. Because the NL is 25 years older, it is sometimes called the "Senior Circuit," and the AL is called the "Junior Circuit."

By the beginning of the twentieth century, baseball had become America's national pastime. By 1922, professional baseball had become so significant to the country that the United States Supreme Court actually got involved with it, ruling that professional baseball couldn't be regulated under federal antitrust law as interstate business. In a unanimous opinion, the Court held that organized baseball played for money was a sport rather than a business because it was based on "personal effort." To this day, MLB is the only professional sport to have a federal antitrust exemption.

The Court's opinion was written by Chief Justice Oliver Wendell Holmes, Jr., a Civil War veteran who had played amateur baseball in his youth. As an aside having nothing to do with baseball, Justice Holmes holds another interesting distinction: In 1864, on the outskirts of Washington, D.C., he probably saved Abraham Lincoln from being shot by Confederate soldiers when the President exposed himself to enemy fire by climbing up on some defensive works. Holmes, then a young Union officer with significant combat experience, didn't recognize the President, and perhaps injudiciously (or perhaps not, given what was otherwise about to happen) bellowed out "Get down, you damn fool!" If there is a moral to the story, I guess it would be that interesting people from all walks of life have made different and unexpected contributions to our national game; also, know when to duck.

Except for a couple of years, since 1903 the best teams in the NL and the AL have met yearly for a post-season play-off, the World Series, to determine the best team in baseball. (Until 1997, NL teams and AL teams did not play against each other during the regular season; they only met during the World Series.) Calling something that is primarily American a "World Series" may seem a bit over the top to folks from other countries or for those who didn't grow up with the game. Even though professional baseball is being played all over the world, the term "World Series" still seems fitting. MLB in the United States attracts the best baseball players from every country, and baseball fans everywhere know that MLB stars play at the highest professional level anywhere. Baseball fans also know what it means for a team to win the World Series.

Professional baseball may have a bucolic origin, but it came of age in the eastern cities of the United States during the industrial revolution of the late nineteenth and early twentieth centuries. People were immigrating to the United States from many places, and from what I've read, life in America's urban centers of the time could be grim. Imagine how wonderful it must have been for these people to get away for an afternoon to a beautiful emerald expanse, not unlike the one my brother-in-law recalled as his earliest memory of going to a minor league ball field in Indianapolis. Not only the game itself, but also the pastoral setting, may have had a part in making the experience so popular.

MLB largely stayed east of the Mississippi River until the late 1950s. Each February, teams would come together down in the southeastern states for Spring Training. The MLB regular season would begin in early April, and go until October. Back then, there weren't as many teams, and whichever team won the most games was the champion (or "Pennant Winner") of its league, and went straight to the World Series.

In those days, the teams rode trains or took buses from city to city. After World War II, however, modes of transport changed. Commercial air travel came into its own, and it became easier and quicker to go between major cities. Also, the population in the western states was growing. Two things happened to MLB as a result: several teams that were in eastern cities moved west; and new teams called "Expansion" teams were created. Some of the teams that moved were renamed, and some kept their original names. At present, there are thirty MLB teams based in cities all over the United States and Canada. With so many teams, the old league organizational structures became unwieldy. Even with modern air travel, it made sense for teams to play other teams somewhat nearby: it was easier for fans to attend the games, there was less wear and tear on players from time zone changes, and proximity helped preserve traditional rivalries. Accordingly, MLB organized each league into three divisions along geographic lines, with five teams in each division. The current setup looks like this:

National League

East Division ("NL East")

> Braves (Atlanta, Georgia)
> Marlins (Miami, Florida)
> Mets (Queens, New York City, New York)
> Nationals (Washington, DC)
> Phillies (Philadelphia, Pennsylvania)

Central Division ("NL Central")

> Brewers (Milwaukee, Wisconsin)
> Cardinals (St. Louis, Missouri)
> Cubs (Chicago, Illinois)
> Reds (Cincinnati, Ohio)
> Pirates (Pittsburgh, Pennsylvania)

West Division ("NL West")

> Diamondbacks (Phoenix, Arizona)
> Dodgers (Los Angeles, California)
> Giants (San Francisco, California)
> Padres (San Diego, California)
> Rockies (Denver, Colorado)

American League

East Division ("AL East")

> Blue Jays (Toronto, Canada)
> Orioles (Baltimore, Maryland)
> Rays (Tampa Bay, Florida)
> Red Sox (Boston, Massachusetts)
> Yankees (The Bronx, New York City, New York)

Central ("AL Central")

Indians (Cleveland, Ohio)
Royals (Kansas City, Missouri)
Tigers (Detroit, Michigan)
Twins (Minneapolis, Minnesota)
White Sox (Chicago, Illinois)

West Division ("AL West")

Astros (Houston, Texas)
Athletics (Oakland, California)
Los Angeles Angels of Anaheim (Anaheim,
California)
Mariners (Seattle, Washington)
Rangers (Arlington, Texas)

As I said, at one time the League Champions went straight to the World Series. Now, the journey to the World Series is far more arduous. Ten teams (five from each League) will qualify for the playoffs: the winner of each Division in each League, plus two "wild card" teams (the teams with the best winning records that didn't win their Divisions). The two wild card teams in each League will play one game against each other, and the two winning wild card teams will advance to their respective League's five-game Division Championship Series. The two teams in each League that win their Division Championship Series will play a seven-game series for their League Championship: the National League Championship Series ("NLCS"), and the American League Championship Series (the "ALCS"). Only then, after having possibly played twelve post-season games, will the survivors get to play for the World Series Championship.

Earlier, when I discussed batting, I mentioned that the AL, unlike the NL, has the Designated Hitter rule.

Beginning in 1997, AL teams and NL teams started playing each other, to a limited extent, during the regular season. During interleague play, the DH rule is in effect when the home team is an AL team; conversely, it is not in effect when the home team is an NL team.

There are potentially seven games in the World Series. These games are played in the stadiums of the two League Champions in a 2-3-2 format. The DH rule is in effect in games played in the AL Champion's stadium, but not in games played in the NL Champion's stadium. Since the World Series may go to seven games, one team will get the "home-field" advantage of possibly playing four games (the first two and the last two) of the series in its stadium. Through 2002, the home-field advantage alternated yearly; one year the AL Champion had the home-field advantage, the next year the NL Champion had it. However, the 2002 All-Star Game ended in a tie, which was most unsatisfactory. Beginning in 2003, the home-field advantage for the World Series has gone to the team in the League that won that year's All-Star Game. Likewise, in both the AL and the NL, the teams with the best records have home-field advantage in their Division Series and League Championship Series. What teams in the two leagues have won the most World Championships? In the AL, the New York Yankees have won 27, and in the NL, the St. Louis Cardinals have won 11.

The All-Star Game has been a prominent feature of the MLB season since 1933. Prior to 2003, All-Star Games were exclusively "exhibition games," meaning that they had no effect (barring player injury) on the outcome of a season. However, as noted above, they now have an impact on the World Series. During the first part of every season, fans get an opportunity to vote (now online and free) their favorite players onto their Leagues'

All-Star team. MLB players and managers also have some say as to which players make the team rosters. Midway through the regular season, MLB takes a few days' break from its grinding 162-game schedule, and the players chosen to represent their respective Leagues travel to the selected city to play the All-Star Game. The city changes yearly, but no matter where, the DH rule is now in effect for every All-Star Game. The two managers of the teams in the World Series the year before are given the honor of managing their respective league's All-Star teams. All-Star Games are a lot of fun, and it is a real honor for a player to be chosen to participate.

Wrapping It Up

Way back in the Preface, I mentioned that my dad had played baseball in his youth, and that he loved the game passionately. That was about all I knew about my family and baseball when I started writing this book. Early in the writing, I told my mom, now in her late eighties, that I had started working on a book about baseball. I was going on about what I had in mind to do, and she looked at me strangely and asked:

"You do know about your grandfather, don't you?"

My grandfather had died in 1933, almost two decades before I was born. All I knew about him was that he had been a railroad engineer in rural North Carolina back in the early days of the twentieth century, so I responded that I knew that he had been a train engineer back in the day.

"You mean your daddy never told you?" she shot back.

"Told me what Momma?"

"That your grandfather killed a man with a baseball."

I was stunned. My father had never once mentioned this to me. My mom went on:

"Yes Johnny, he used to talk about it with me all the time. It was back in the 1900s. It happened at one of those games between town teams that the boys used to play on the weekends down South. Your grandfather was pitching, and he threw a pitch and hit a man in the head and killed him. It was an accident, and your grandfather didn't mean to do it, but your daddy said that your grandfather never picked up a baseball again after that."

It didn't take me too long after that conversation to figure out that this was (1) the reason my father had never encouraged me to be a pitcher, and (2) why he never played catch with me again after accidentally popping me in the head with the baseball that evening over half a century ago. My dad didn't want me to have to live with what he had grown up with, and although he passed away in 1990, if he's somewhere looking over my shoulder as I write this, I want him to know that I love and respect him all the more for having shielded me from knowledge of this accident.

I also found out that my grandfather and my father weren't the only ones in my family who loved and played baseball. By most accounts, the best player of all was my cousin, Dr. William Morris Britt ("Bill," or "Billy" until he went away to the Army). As I mentioned, Daddy was an orphan. He was raised by his uncle, Bill's father, back in the 1930s; so I see Bill more as my uncle than my cousin. Bill was long and lean, athletic, and one heck of a pitcher. Bill pitched for his high school and college teams, and on local teams around Rowland, North Carolina, the small town near where he and my father grew up. Bill signed a minor league contract with the

Philadelphia (now Oakland) Athletics organization, but his mother decreed that he would finish his education first—then life got in the way, and Bill never got back to professional baseball.

However, my favorite story about Bill was how, back in the days of segregation, players on a local black baseball team would come on Saturday morning and help him get his farm chores done so that he could pitch for their team that afternoon—the only white player on either team! I'm proud that young Billy did that, at a time and in a place where it wasn't easy. Sadly, Bill passed away as I was rounding third and heading for home with this book. In a twist of fate, on the afternoon of the day Bill died I happened to be at Dodger Stadium watching the best MLB game I've ever seen.

My grandpa and my daddy, and then Bill, were in the back of my mind as I worked to get this book done. But there is much more to baseball for me than my family's ties to the game. Baseball is an American game; we invented it, but people all over the world have opened themselves to it, come to love it, and have made the game their own. In a time of change, uncertainty, and strife, we can go to a ballpark and share in the joy of something familiar that ties us together, no matter where we came from or how much we have. Yes, I have come to love this game, and writing this book has opened my eyes to how much baseball means to me. Thank you for letting me share a few hours of your day, and for letting me tell you about baseball.

ACKNOWLEDGMENTS

Anyone who claims that he could write a book like this without help is not telling the truth. I had lots of help. First, I would like to thank my wife, Sandy. Without her gentle and loving guidance, this book would not have happened. I am doubly blessed because she is a former English teacher, and her editing saved me from the more outrageous grammatical errors and linguistic excesses that I would otherwise have insisted be included in this book. I would also like to thank Ryan Hinson, a professional colleague, whose baseball knowledge and attention to detail helped keep me on the base path. Rounding out my immediate support team are Ramy Kassabgui, who assisted me with the illustrations and other technical issues, and Matt Miller, who helped put together my website, www.casualfansguide.com. In addition, I deeply appreciate the efforts of the good folks at Xulon Press in shepherding my book to market.

There are many others who offered their valuable insights and comments, and/or read my book before its publication, including, in alphabetical order:

Louie Adame
Steve Behar
Roger Boudreau

Michael Clampitt
Peter Del Greco
David Evans
Kim Haack
Bill "Bones" Hannan
Rebecca Jorne
Joe Kempf
Jeremy Kollitz
Frank Malinoski
Andrew Petillon
Karol Pollock
David Van Havermaat

I would especially like to acknowledge Knute Salhus. Knute is a life-long New York Yankees fan, who many years ago took me to the original Yankee Stadium. Knute opened his veins, bled blue and white pinstripes, and taught me so much. Also, I am indebted to the greatest baseball announcer who ever called a game, Edward Vincent "Vin" Scully. I learn something new about baseball every time I listen to him.

Finally, I would like to thank our beautiful grandchildren, Joshua and Zoe, for inspiring us to finish this book. Always know that Grandma and Grandpa John love you.

INDEX

$\mathbf{B}$elow is an index listing significant terms and expressions used in this book—some used multiple times. Rather than list each page where the word or term appears, I have selected the page number(s) where that term or expression is primarily defined or discussed.

About the Author

John Britt was born in the South, but grew up an Air Force brat, living all over the United States and in England. He graduated from the University of California at Berkeley with a B.A. in Political Science (well, of course!) in the 1970s, and then earned law degrees from Loyola Law School, Los Angeles, and Georgetown Law School. Since 1984, he has served as an attorney with the United States Securities and Exchange Commission.

CPSIA information can be obtained at www.ICGtesting.com
Printed in the USA
BVOW020411040413

317229BV00005B/10/P